The Secrets of
Master Marketing

DAVID L. HANCOCK

The Secrets of Master Marketing

David L. Hancock

2003

DAVID L. HANCOCK

The Secrets of Master Marketing

DAVID L. HANCOCK

I would like to express my appreciation for the dedication my wife Susan has given to me in the publishing of this book. Without her understanding and support this book would not have been possible.

DAVID L. HANCOCK

Table of Contents

DAVID L. HANCOCK

Thank you for your interest!

*"The amateur salesperson sells products; the
professional sells solutions to needs and problems."*
- Stephen R. Covey

Welcome to "The Secrets of Master
Marketing!"

This book is jam packed with
powerful marketing secrets that will help
you and your business enhance its image and
increase its business... Effortlessly!

I'm certain that these secrets will
dramatically impact your results, and I mean

that. After 11 years of experience in sales and marketing, and the last 8 years of my career dedicated to the mortgage industry, these techniques can become a huge benefit to sales professionals of all types. In fact, I've even referenced other industries to illustrate that they can be applicable in concept to every industry, every product or service, and every profession.

Please enjoy, and I thank you for your interest! Email me today with your suggestions or comments!

To your success!
David L. Hancock
The Marketing Master™
www.DavidLHancock.com
david@davidlhancock.com

Caution

This cleverly disguised book contains the core secrets based on The Marketing Master™ concept – a set of powerfully effective secrets that have turned many average Loan Originators into Master Originators. These ideas are offered to you here for a moderate investment that, if applied properly, will surely return your investment a thousand times over!

You may have purchased this book in hopes to find more business or to reach a comfortable plateau, or you may be like many who want clients to come banging down their doors. But whether you want a little or a lot of business, these secrets are so simple that they can be easily applied by any Sales Professional. Simply put, they work over and over!

You're learning from someone who's done it the hard way. I am continually on the frontlines, day after day, doing what most of you are trying to do – and that's getting more business. I have oftentimes failed miserably, but I have also reached many phenomenal successes. And these secrets are the result of years of wisdom-building, trial-and-error experience. Believe me, they are far from being mere hot air!

While these secrets are tried and proven, they do, however, require some work on your part. In other words, many of these systems are generic in nature and will require some time and creative effort for your specific application, but not so much that they are too vague or require a lot of investment. They simply are tools to help you build your own unique style and thus create endless streams of new, repeat, and referral business for yourself. They do so because they all come back to one basic, fundamental marketing principle, which is that of The Marketing Master™!

The days of knocking on – and sometimes down – doors, to get business are long gone, let alone just to get people's attention. Long gone are the days of using the telephone so much that your ear starts to morph itself into the headset. And long gone are the days of constantly begging your customers to give you the table scraps of their business. In other words, prospecting is out. Positioning is in.

So, let's get started. However, before we begin, a warning here is needed. It's been my experience that some of you reading this book wish to project a certain image about yourselves or about your businesses in the marketplace. More concerned with looking good than making money, your ego may often end up in the way of following these practical steps and, consequently, making the money you truly deserve.

Others among you are probably used to traditional, MBA-style, statistical analytical types of knock-until-you-drop marketing approaches. For you, my "street-wise" secrets may just rub you the wrong way. I am not implying that they are too aggressive, or too far out there. Far from it. They are, however, practical and extremely effective secrets that are essential to not only survive, but also thrive in today's increasingly hyper-competitive marketplace.

If you want more business, then read on! These secrets will help you do just that in a powerful way. Follow these 10 secrets if you will, but ignore them at your own risk!

Top-Of-Mind Awareness

Before we begin, you must understand the concepts that will follow. In today's society, we have experienced two major shifts that have revolutionized the entire business landscape. The first and most important one is competition. The mere fact that business is becoming increasingly hyper-competitive is truly an understatement. The Mortgage Industry alone is growing at an explosive rate.

The business boom is far from being just a boom. And the reason for this stems from the second shift that has taken place,

which is information. Along with the
eruption in multi-channel broadcasting,
digital technology, and cellular
telecommunications, the Internet is
skyrocketing with every single minute! The
ability to retrieve information in nanosecond
speed has caused entire layers of middle
managers in huge corporations to fall the
way of the dinosaurs. The information age
notwithstanding, with more and more
employers facing disgruntled employees in
today's highly litigious atmosphere, jobs are
soon becoming things of the past.

So, what does all this mean? It means
that, for a person or business to be able to
remain in business, marketing strategies
must be such that it places that person or
business at the top of prospects' minds at all
times. It is not so much to look for more
business, but to be the business of choice.
For every category of business that exists,
there are thousands of competitors fighting
for the same market. And since the
information revolution in today's
knowledge-based economy has helped to
educate people on what's available, there's
no longer a need to prospect for and

persuade people to have them "buy into" an idea.

The goal, nowadays, is to be the one from whom they do business with – among all other possibilities. Marketing must therefore be such that when a prospect needs a particular product, one name comes to their minds in an instant. In other words, positioning is a process by which a psychological "anchor" has been placed into the minds of prospects so that they come to choose one specific person or company over another.

"Top-of-mind awareness" is a term originally coined by Ellis Verdi, the once president of the National Retail Advertisers Council and owner of a prestigious marketing and advertising agency in New York. He said that what most people wrongfully seek to accomplish in their promotional efforts is to get cash flow and not results. And they usually accomplish this by offering sales, promotions, discounts, and price reductions. As he said at a recent conference, "Discounting is like a drug. It brings in some business, and for some it may even bring in a lot of business. But the effect usually wears off and the company will soon find itself with the need to discount further in order to create more business, let alone to stay in it."

Top-of-mind awareness, however, is such that with it there is no need to use price-based promotional methods. What it does is two things: 1) It psychologically impacts people so that the mere mention and knowledge of one's company, product, or service inherently creates a need for them, and 2) it places one at the top of a specific market's consciousness so that one is instantly chosen when people want what that person or business has to offer.

"Master Positioning" is a term I've coined that stands for a perfect blend of the art of positioning and the science of direct response – the result of creating top-of-mind positioning in order to turn you, your business, or your products into powerful magnets. The following secrets all reflect this powerful concept – one so simple and yet remarkably more effective, more affordable, and of course more effortless, than any other marketing secret imagined.

Do Not Copy

If there's one problem in all advertising, marketing, and promotional efforts, it is the sheer fact that there is too much competition out there. Everything just seems the same. If one copies another company, let alone another company's promotional efforts, it only serves as a reminder of one's competition. Therefore, you don't want to remind your prospects about your competition, do you? So, don't copy them. As Earl Nightingale once said, "Don't copy, create!" Be unique. Be original. Be special. Be so different that your name as well as the name of the services you deliver become generic in the minds of prospects.

Have you ever heard a doctor say: "Take two acetylsalicylic acid tablets and call me in the morning"? What about "facial tissue," "cotton swab" or "adhesive bandage"? Of course not! Its Aspirin, Kleenex, Q-Tip, and Band-Aid. And that's not all. Xerox, FedEx, Velcro, Copy Max and Quick Lube also stick like glue in the mind. How is this possible? While there are many reasons for this, the first one is the fact that many of these firms created not only a new product or service but also a whole new category to place them in (see the next secret).

For now, let's stick to the idea of "uniqueness". This concept might seem far-fetched for the type of product or service you offer, but in reality it really isn't. As expressed earlier, top-of-mind awareness is the greatest key to marketing success in all facets and types of business. Top-of-mind positioning is a process by which an "anchor" in the subconscious of prospects has been created and through which you position yourself or your product above all other choices.

For instance, when deciding to find out about the type of product or service you provide, let alone when deciding to buy what you offer your name or the name of your business or product must come to your prospects' minds instantaneously. How is this done? Well, there are several ways to accomplish this, but let me share at least two of them with you.

The first and most important is names (or in other words, packaging). Does your product or service name intrinsically reflect the type of service you offer and does so instantaneously? If not, you might want to reconsider renaming your product or service (even your company name). For example, if I told you "Copy Max", you will automatically think of a company offering copies. You might say, "Yeah, but that's only for big chains with big budgets!" I have heard this many times over. My answer usually is, "But how do you think they became large chains anyway?"

Today, it amazes me to see companies with names that mean absolutely nothing, such as acronyms (like "XYZ Enterprises") or names that do not reflect the competitive advantage if not at least the nature of the business. If you are a computer network consultant, are you called "Fred's' Consulting" or are you called "Practical Technologies"? What's better: "John's Dry-Cleaners" or "Spotless Cleaners"? You see the name of your firm or product/service should intrinsically reflect what you do, what you offer, and how you are different from your competition – in just a few words. Some may not have the ability to change your firms name; however you could suggest product or services to be appropriately named.

This generally requires a great deal of creative skill. When refining a business's corporate identity, or product line, some names will pop instantly into the mind while others take more time and effort. So, here's a helpful hint: try writing down as many names as possible – at least 20 – and pass it around among friends, family, and acquaintances. Ask them what pulls them the most. Look for the "Aha's!" or the "Wow's!" These are the ones you want.

If not, either you will have one or two that stick out, or words from a combination of two or three of your names that can be used together wonderfully. Listen to what your circle of influence has to say, but also read between their lines. In other words, many people will tell you what they think looks best, but remember that your goal is not to look better, but to get busier. Watch their facial expressions when they read your names. Ask them a few hours later what stuck in their minds and not just the ones they remembered as being the ones they liked best.

However, I must point out that there are exceptions to this rule. For example, if you are self-employed, or home-based and don't use a fictitious name at all , you may also be limited financially, since repositioning a business is sometimes not an inexpensive process – particularly if your name is already established in the marketplace. In these cases, a second technique can help; add a tagline to your name. A tagline is a small sentence, preferably five words or less, that complements your name and says it all in one single swoop. I'm sure you've heard of "Enjoy the Ride" (Nissan), "Fights Cavities" (Crest), "Kills Bugs Dead" (Raid), or "The Midas Touch" (Midas). You can do this with any name.

One successful originator added some flair to his name by using a tagline in all his marketing pieces (ads, letterhead, business cards, media and promo kits, etc), which read: "Paul 'The Crunchman' Clemmons" Another Originating Team calls themselves "The Debt Free Express" on radio and print advertising. Whether you have a unique name or not, add a tagline to your name that truly communicates all that you are.

Make sure to use your tagline in all your communications, promotional pieces, as well as standard stationery. Additionally, every single aspect of your operations – even breathing! – should in itself become a fundamental marketing process. Remember to look at every aspect of your business, whether it's answering your phone, (recognize mine "This is David, I can help you!"), writing your invoices, mailing your brochures, and even handing out your business cards. It should all become part of a marketing approach in which it emphasizes your uniqueness through your special name or tagline.

For example, do you have an answering machine message that says: "Sorry, but I'm not here to take your call right now"? Ugh! Don't do that. Make your machine work for you. Change it to something like: "You've reached David Hancock, 'The Marketing Master'. I am currently coaching someone on 'The Secrets of Master Marketing', designed for Loan Originators seeking to explode their business. If you wish to leave a message, please include your name and telephone number after the tone. Thanks for your interest!' (Beep)"

In the above example, several other secrets are followed. We will deal with these aspects in greater detail later in the book, but for now just realize that everything you do must become a part of creating top-of-mind awareness. You don't need a huge advertising budget to make this work. Once you've got this down, use it in all your communications. You have to live, sleep, eat, and breathe your new name or tagline. Later I will discuss this a little further, especially with what I call a "Pedestal Calling Card." For now, don't copy. Be unique!

Appoint Yourself

A recently understood segment of marketing is the immense power behind categories. Often, many businesses build their entire marketing strategy around a particular brand and its "better" qualities, only to have it all go down the drain in the end.

Remember the "New Coke"? In the 80's, Pepsi conducted taste tests they called "The Pepsi Challenge." Coke heard from their research that a newer, better tasting brand would take the market by storm. Three years later, not only were they forced to reintroduce the older version under the banner "Coca-Cola Classic," but they also had to eventually wipe the new Coke out. "Better" is not always better.

The originators of the "category" concept are Jack Trout and Al Ries, the fathers of positioning. In their excellent book "The 22 Immutable Laws of Marketing", they made what I believe to be the most powerful notion ever conceived in the world of business, in that marketing is not a battle of products but a battle of perceptions. My mentor also used to tell me that "Perceived truth is more powerful than truth itself", and I certainly agree. For instance, a large airline company conducted a survey among passengers. And to the question, "If your food trays were dirty, would you assume that the airline also does poor maintenance on its engines", the answer was (as illogical as it sounds) "yes" for an overwhelming majority! Marketing is all about perception.

Look at the leaders in your organization or field. Are they famous because they're busy, or are they busy because they're famous? For example, a particular mortgage guru is one of the first authors in the America to professionalize and personalize the origination industry and has been instrumental in the popularization of "Power to Be Your Best" marketing.

In addition to the fact that he maintains a portfolio of highly successful clients, this guru is still widely recognized among the mortgage public to be one of the best originators, whether he is indeed the best or not. However, sales, like mortgage origination, are a matter of personable ability and not of seniority – let alone fame. But you see, when people perceive that you are the best, it is much more powerful than actually being the best. Perceived truth is definitely more powerful than truth itself.

If you have a product that is the best or that you perceive as being the best, it may not be a shared perception among your target market. However, whether your product is better than your competition or not, if it's perceived as the leader in its field or category, people will automatically assume that it's the best. People will often say, "They must be the best because they're the leaders!" Why? People have the natural tendency to gravitate towards the leader of a given category. They automatically conclude that the leader is indeed the best. For example, Coke outsells Pepsi, even though in taste tests Pepsi seems to be the better tasting brand.

Now, all of this is fine and dandy, but you're probably wondering at this point how you can accomplish this. Before I show you how to do that, let me give you an example. If I asked you 'who was the third person to fly over the Atlantic in a solo flight?' many of you are not history buffs and would more than likely be stumped with that one. However, most of you know that Lindbergh was the first person to fly solo over the Atlantic. Being the first, he comes to mind immediately. So, rather than ask you who was the third person to fly over the Atlantic, if I asked you the same question but rephrased in another way, as in "Who was the first woman to fly over the Atlantic in a solo flight?" Of course, it's Amelia Earhart.

This is the power of self-appointment. One of my favorite marketing gurus is Dan Kennedy, author of the bestsellers "No B.S. Business Success" and "No B.S. Sales Success." He stresses, "You don't need someone else's permission to become successful." When it comes to marketing, he is absolutely right! Many people try to compete and may even get the first secret down pat, but where they often fail is in creating top-of-mind positioning by drowning their image in a currently known category.

Everybody knows who is the first in one category or another, but rarely do people remember who's second, let alone third. And one of the biggest faults businesspeople have is in attempting to market themselves as a better business, with a better product or service, or better rates. Let me share with you a secret that might shock you – if I haven't done it already: Nobody cares. Nobody cares if you're the best or number one... Nobody! Even when people say they have chosen one business over another because they have a better product, they only think they do and were initially attracted to that particular business for other reasons – probably at a subconscious level. If they do make a choice based on a business's superior qualities, they will not stay with that business for long, for they will quickly jump at the next "best" thing that comes along.

People want the newest, the latest, the fastest, the freshest, the brightest, etc. They want the leading product or service in any given field. They want the best! And when I say that they want the "best", I don't necessarily mean the "best" but what people perceive as being the "best." So, what do you do in order to produce this effect? If there's no category you can be first in, create one. As Dan Kennedy said, you don't need other people's permission to do that. Creating your very own category is powerful because it is impossible for your competition to copy you.

You can be the first to cater to a specific market, the first to offer an alternative to an existing product or service, or the first to cater to a market in a unique way – such as by offering an ordinary product or service but with a unique twist. You can also customize a general product or service for a specific market. For instance, look at your background or your clients – is there a common thread? Are there any special awards you or your products have won? Are there any unique references or endorsements you can obtain from local celebrities? Do you or your company possess any unique accreditation, certifications, or memberships in specific groups?

You might be a mortgage consultant that caters exclusively to financial institutions and planners – you're biggest clientele. You might market yourself as "the first to serve the financially inclined", "the leader in mortgage solutions for bankers", "we take the risk out of mortgages for those who deal with it everyday", "the financier's mortgage consultant", or "the first mortgage consultant for the smart investor". Don't be the best in some category. Be the first in one!

Before we go to the next secret, I must share with you a small tip that is relevant to both the two first secrets. Do you have what is called a pedestal calling card or speech? And if so, does it create instant, top-of-mind position? A pedestal calling card is what you say when you introduce yourself and usually includes a sentence or two (30 words or less) that states concisely and effectively who you are and what you do. How do you do that? Think benefits. Why should your clients hire you? Why should they buy from you? Why should they even listen to you? And better still, why should they remember you at all?

When you introduce yourself to people, do give your name and tell people what you do? If you do, please take this advice: You must stop it right now! I know, I know. You're probably thinking, "What? He wants me to stop telling people what I do? But how will they know who I am, let alone remember me?" Before we go further, let me explain what I mean.

Ever heard of the "Mustard Principle"? Let's say you've just met a salesperson and, after introducing himself, he gives you a sales presentation. Everything is perfect. He is dressed absolutely impeccably, gave a stunning spiel, and conducted a first-class meeting with you. But all throughout the encounter, you couldn't help but notice that he had a little spot on his tie, a little mustard stain if you will. Two weeks later, however, if I would ask you, "What do you remember most about your meeting with this man?" More than likely, the first thing that would pop into your mind would be – yes, you guessed it – the mustard stain!

Now, as the old saying goes, "You never get a second chance to make a good first impression!" That statement is not only true but it also applies even to the simplest of things, such as names. How often have you met people only to forget their names only moments later? So, the bottom-line is for you or your business to stick in the minds of the people you've just met. Again, your introduction is not meant to persuade this potential client (or potential referral of clients) to do business with you. The trick is to have you in your prospects' consciousness at all times.

Therefore, when you introduce yourself to others, use your unique name, your tagline, your unique category, and the benefits you provide – and not just your name, the name of your firm, and what you do. For instance, don't say, "Hello, my name is David Hancock; I'm an Account Executive" or "I'm a Mortgage Consultant."

Rather, say, "My name is David Hancock, the 'Marketing Master™'. I help turn mortgage offices into profit centers." (By the way, that's my pedestal speech!)

Not only will it arouse interest but it will also make your name stick in their minds, which is what you really want. That person will either remember you when needing what you have to offer, refer you to others when the opportunity presents itself, or talk about you openly especially when others bring up the subject. That's the power of what I call "Super Glue for the Mind!"

Here are other examples. If you're a mortgage consultant specializing in VA solutions, don't say, "My name is Jane Doe and I am a mortgage consultant" or "I specialize in VA financing." Instead, say, "My name is Jane Doe of 'VA Magic" I help our armed services and veterans relieve their home ownership headaches." Don't say, "My name is John Doe; I am a management consultant specializing in accounting processes." Rather, say, "My name is John Doe of 'A Knack with Knumbers'. I help cut a firm's expenses of time, effort, and money in half by simplifying their accounting systems." Now, do you see the difference?

This in itself puts you in a whole different category, but I must stress the importance of being the leader in a category and using it in all your communications, especially when giving your pedestal speech. If you're not the first in some category or another, be the first in one you've created.

DAVID L. HANCOCK

Make The Ordinary Extraordinary

So, if you're following the secrets, you should now have a unique name, possibly a tagline, and established yourself as the first or leader in your unique category. What about the service or product you offer? Do you offer an extraordinary product or service, or an ordinary one? You see, even if the service you provide is customary, most likely traditional, and probably offered by your competition, you should make it appear unique just as well.

Remember that perception is more powerful than truth. You don't need to emphasize that your product or service is unique, better than the competition, or even the best for that matter. Trying to do so or declaring that it is can sometimes be worse than not saying anything at all. The reason for that is it makes you appear as if you are bluffing, or exaggerating at best.

For instance, if you told people that you're product or service is number one in the marketplace, your clients will probably either laugh at you or at least question your statement. But if you put a name on your product or service (and trademark it if possible), you will indirectly cast an aura of exclusivity and superiority and do so without utterly flaunting it.

By the way, please note that unique trademarks don't need to be registered, unless you are looking for financial compensation if someone ever copies you. In that case, you must go through a trademark attorney to register your name or names. I am not an attorney and please do not consider this as legal advice. I strongly recommend that you see a trademark or corporate attorney for assistance in this area, especially if you're seeking to completely prevent any form of piracy.

However, once you've conducted a thorough search and found that your trademark is indeed original, and after formally registering your trademark, you will be able to use the "®" symbol (registered trademark) rather than the "™" in all your communications – and keep copycats at bay, or even sue them should they ever use your names or taglines.

Nevertheless, always keep in mind that perception is powerful. When it comes to the perception of a product or service, it will generally fall into one of three categories. (This is especially true with services since they are intangible.) The first one is the "customary," the second is the "assumed," and the third is the "unique". Let's take a look at each element in more detail.

The Customary

You might be a mortgage consultant offering pre-qualifications to home buyers as part of your portfolio to your real estate agents, a service that is also widely offered by most mortgage consultants these days. However, don't just leave it like that. Say, "Ask us about our special 'Total Home Buying Tranquility' service." If you're a dry-cleaner offering a tie cleaning service (as most dry-cleaners do), don't just call it a "tie cleaning service," call it a special name, as in "Bring your ties out of retirement with our 'Re-TIE-rement Reversal' process".

Before we go any further, I know what you may be thinking right now. You're probably thinking that you are a professional businessperson representing a high class, high quality product or service, and that this type of strategy is too "hokey" or that it doesn't apply to you. When I started out in business, I was a business development consultant specializing in customized new home construction and solutions. Dealing with a very professional clientele, I heard this type of objection all the time. However, I still say that it is possible for you to use this technique, even in these circumstances.

For example, one day, while looking through the yellow pages I was immediately struck by an ad from a particular dentist who specializes in pain and anxiety management. He has an anesthetist on staff, and uses intravenous and general sedation for his patients in order to make the process of dental work a more comfortable experience. Most dentists offer this "ordinary" service. But what did his ad say? The headline was made up of two simple words: "Dream Dentistry". Now that's good!

In essence, even if your service is customary or your competition offers the same thing you do, by putting a name on an often-nameless product, you cast an aura of uniqueness and superiority instantaneously without having to state it outright. As one of my mentors used to say to me, "Implication is more powerful than specification!" The resulting effect is the fact that not only will the name keep you in the back of the minds of your prospects, but it will also create curiosity, arouse interest, and enhance desire. By and large, if people had to choose between a general product or service and one that, through its name, implies a better or more unique kind of product or service (some kind of added value), more than likely they will go for the second option.

For instance, if you owned an imported car that needed a brake job, whom would you choose: A general mechanic? Or one who specializes in imported cars by marketing its service as "Are your brakes screaming in a different language? Come and see us for your 'Quicker-than-Customs' foreign car brake inspection"? You get the picture. (Oops! I'm getting ahead of myself again, since this example also reflects Secret #4, which is the power of specialization. But I guess you're getting used to me by now, right? 'Enough said.)

The Assumed

Speaking of mechanics, are you a mechanic and, as normal practice, offer free estimates? If you are a mechanic, you most likely do. Those that don't are rare. Everybody expects free estimates from mechanics or garages these days. However, as simple as it may sound, if you specify what is usually taken for granted, you make your name stick! For example, you might call your free estimate "The Hassle Free

Formula" or the "No Greater than Guesstimate Estimate." Your tagline could even be "Where Smiles and Estimates are Free!"

You see, it might sound silly, but the attractiveness of this process is so simple. People may or may not know that garages offer free estimates and, more often than not, they only assume that they do. But with a service name in which people are told that their estimates are free, they are now assured that particular garage offers free estimates. In other words, you're turning an assumed service into an assured service in the minds of people. And in this day and age where people no longer have the time to shop around, when they'll need the services of a mechanic your name will pop into their minds instantaneously.

This technique is indeed remarkably effective and can easily be customized for a number of mortgage solutions as well like debt analysis or prequals, etc.

As shown in the previous example, making the ordinary extraordinary is like turning the assumed into the assured. In fact, there is an immense power behind guarantees, and I love marketing on this remarkable concept. Some people think that guarantees are outdated, overused, and ineffective. Others think that they are not necessary. I know for a fact it's not true.

People not only love guarantees, but as I said earlier, in today's hypercompetitive marketplace you need to stand out. And a good way to do this is by offering a guarantee in one form or another so that, when placed side-by-side with a competitor, you will be the one who's chosen. Guarantees sometimes frighten businesspeople because it involves taking a great risk on the part of the entrepreneur. The possible loss of revenue is indeed a frightening idea for many people. But if you have a good product, have had good experience with it, and believe in it wholeheartedly, guarantees can become powerful weapons in building your business.

In fact, guarantees help to reduce complaints. Why? They are often perceived as an expression of confidence in the product or service. With scams and crooks now rampant in the marketplace, people have a tendency to forgive far more easily businesses that have shown to believe in their products. Therefore, guarantees not only increase sales but also communicate confidence, credibility, and of course superiority – as in superior customer service.

However, if you still feel that you cannot offer guarantees or if your type of work stops you from doing so, there are three key areas here you may want to consider. First, does your product or service provide a result that is quantifiable and measurable? Second, can your product or service be easily replaced or exchanged? And third, do you offer additional products or services outside your core portfolio that you can provide in order to satisfy your client?

If you're not prepared to give a full-money back guarantee, you might want to consider adding or subtracting something instead. Here are some examples. You're a mortgage consultant offering seminars to real estate agents to increase productivity. You might want to offer a guarantee that promises an increase in your agent's sales results by, say, 25% following your seminar. If your agent's sales force doesn't meet this goal within a specific period of time, you could offer an additional seminar (or one-on-one consulting, perhaps telephone consulting) free of charge.

You may be a mortgage consultant that is compensated on a percentage of the loan size. As a name for your guarantee, you may want to call it the "Risk Reverser" guarantee. Additionally, you might give a bonus product or service free of charge as a way to thank your client for their business. In this case, don't just offer it as a standard part of your package. Market it in the form of a guarantee. If, for instance, you are a project management consultant in the computer field, you could add a bonus-training seminar to be conducted after your consulting contract is completed in order to guarantee that people implement and maintain your recommendations effectively. You can call it the "After-Project Assurance" guarantee or the "Perfect Project Pledge."

In essence, the idea is to guarantee in the minds of prospects, that which is a generally assumed part of your business. If the prospect perceives that doing business with you has added value, even if that which you offer is identical to your competition or included in a total package, you will be able to destroy your competition easily! Very often, however, the problem not only lies with what prospects perceive but also with what businesspeople perceive. They too wrongfully assume that parts of their products or services are not important, that marketing them is unnecessary, or as one client of mine once said, that "it all comes with the territory". I'm sure you've heard the old joke about what happens when you assume... you get the picture.

By the way, that client of mine specializes in debt management and financial planning that follows up with his clients after closing to ensure implementation and doesn't bill them for these seemingly "ordinary" services. In fact, these additional small steps are common practice throughout the entire financial service community. I asked him to put a name on it. He now calls it his post closing "Client Progress Program". Remember, if you turn the ordinary into the extraordinary, you will turn ordinary marketing into extraordinary results.

The Unique

Above all, you may still be offering some very special or unique service that your competition doesn't offer at all. That's great! However, the same rule applies here. Don't just leave it to a vague title or description. Put a name on it and christen your unique service, even if it's not entirely new. For instance, if you're a mortgage consultant offering seminars on how to get the most out of a particular construction to perm product you've customized and the company endorses your efforts, call it the "Construction Savvy in a Cinch Seminar."

In fact, while having a unique product or service beats the previous two categories in creating top-of-mind positioning, it doesn't have to be an entirely new thing. It can be copied and customized in such a way that it appears unique or new. According to Brian Tracy in his program "The Psychology of Selling," many people have made fortunes by simply improving a current product or service by merely packaging it in an entirely different way. Remember the "pet rock"?

This goes back to the issue of the power of perception. I once watched an Oprah Winfrey Show in which Oprah did an interesting piece on marketing. She conducted an apple juice taste test in malls across the United States. While I believe the program was related to how people could be mislead through marketing, she was focusing particularly on how companies can easily use false or misleading advertising. The test revealed some interesting facts nonetheless.

She had two bottles of apple juice. One was a plain, white plastic container with a label donning a picture of an apple. Very plain. Nothing fancy. The second bottle, however, was an intricately shaped glass bottle carrying a red label with the picture of a woman preparing apple juice in her kitchen. When people were asked which apple juice tasted better, the majority said that the juice from the glass bottle with the red label tasted better. The surprise came when she announced to her audience that the juices from both bottles were exactly the same!

Not bad, isn't it? But it didn't stop there. When she asked her participants why they chose the juice from the red-labeled bottle, their answers were astonishing. They said, "It tastes really good", "it's much better than the other one", "it's sweeter tasting", or "it has more flavor". When asked why, one said: "The picture of the lady preparing the juice in her kitchen indicates to me that more care and attention was given into making it, so it has to be better".

It all boils down to perceived truth, which is indeed more powerful than truth itself. So, when it comes to your unique product or service, pay close attention to how you package it or, in other words, to the name and description you put on it. This is how brand names have become generic in the minds of people.

The key is to market your "original" product or service in such a way so that, if it is ever copied, your product or service's name remains firmly fixed in the marketplace and that your competitor's attempt to copy you will only but remind your prospects of you. If you can, add a guarantee or a tagline to your product or service. Ultimately, make your product or service outstanding by making it stand out!

DAVID L. HANCOCK

Find More With Less

The most common mistake newcomers to any field of business make is to think that by expanding their portfolio they will secure more business. Conversely, they think that by narrowing their market they will narrow their chances of getting more business. In either case, nothing can be further from the truth. For instance, a management consultant who I believe had a knack for the human resource arm of the government also offered bookkeeping services, thinking that having more to offer will keep her busier – she then wondered why she wasn't getting any work!

The truth, however, is that specializing your business and narrowing your focus as much as possible will increase your likelihood of getting more business. An accountant specializing in car dealerships will get more business than a general accountant will. An advertising consultant specializing in print media strictly for home furnishing stores will get more business than a typical advertising agent will. A photographer specializing in weddings will get more business than a regular photographer will. And the list goes on and on. See where this is going?

Over the years, this has been referred to as "niche" marketing. Today, niche marketing is increasingly necessary. How is this and what makes it happen? If we go back to the two major shifts I mentioned in the introduction, you'll remember that the explosion in both competition and information are changing the entire business landscape. As more and more businesses get started and more and more people jump into home-based and self-employed opportunities, the less time, energy, and money people will have to spend in choosing those with whom they will do business. This is not only related to new and repeat business but also to referral business.

Let's say you have two friends who are both in car sales, and you're thinking of referring clients to only one of them. One of your friends is a typical car salesperson. The other, however, specializes in first-time car buyers (e.g., students, young drivers, newlyweds, late bloomers, etc). He or she offers special creative financing methods for those new to credit, additional car-specific driver training information for new drivers, and copies of rate comparison charts that suggest insurance companies with the lowest premiums for newly licensed drivers.

Now, let me ask you this question: To whom do you think you will refer more people? This is the awesome power of narrowing one's focus. Think of a laser, which is basically a narrow beam of highly concentrated, amplified light. You want to focus like a laser on your niche and, when you do, you will consequently burn yourself into your prospects' minds.

When you get down to it, as a consumer you will choose, when you have a choice presented to you, to go to a business that specializes in a unique area in which you have a specific need. Specialization, in itself, is a fundamental marketing system, for it casts an aura of superiority and exclusivity. When you deal with a specialist, you will automatically assume that person has greater expertise, has greater knowledge about the field, and offers greater service since, by catering to a unique market, it implies that he or she will have a better understanding of your situation, needs, and concerns. In short, specialization implics superiority.

Niche marketing is the wave of the future. And the greater the competition will become, the greater the need for more specialists. Why do you think there is a trend in specialty stores these days? They are popping up everywhere! Today, there are stores selling only dry foods in bulk. There are vitamin and food supplement stores. There are electronics stores. There are toy stores. There are specialty crafts stores. There are even mothers-to-be and baby-only clothing stores!

The need to specialize is obvious. For example, you can get a toaster from a department store, a home furnishings store, a kitchenware store, a home appliance store, a grocery store, and a drugstore, even a bank! With the competition storming you with information, especially with your very limited time to be able to shop around for the best product at the best price, you will more than likely go the store that pops into your mind the moment you have a need for a toaster. Heck, if there were a store like "Toasters-R-Us," you'd probably go there first!

Nevertheless, your goal is to find your niche, to narrow it down as much as possible, and then to hit it with all you've got. The narrower your market, the more business will come to you. In fact, the narrower your market is, the broader your chances of success in an over communicated, hypercompetitive society will be. It's the paradox of "Find more with Less."

If you're new to business or hesitant about narrowing your focus since you want the ability to offer different products or services, focus on your own specific niche to begin with, and then, as business creates enough cash flow – and confidence – for you, start looking at expanding at that point.

However, be careful. Expansion does not mean extension (see the next secret). If you expand outside of your area of expertise, you will fall down like a house of cards and will have to rebuild from the ground up. We will deal with this further, but for now try to focus on your niche. And as stated in Secret #2, become the specialist by appointing yourself as one!

Divide And Conquer

Core expansion is far different than from extension (shell expansion). Shell expansion is often referred to as franchising, licensing, line extension, or branching out (also known as conglomerating). In this context, I am referring to expansion by division. If you're a specialist in your field – which I hope you will be after reading this book – and you offer only one type of service, you can expand from within by dividing your product or service into multiple, smaller components.

This helps to do three things. 1) It doesn't take away from your category, specialization, or uniqueness. 2) It increases your hit ratio when targeting clients, because some clients might be interested in your entire package while others may be interested in only a portion of it. And 3) it increases the aura of expertise you project because you refrain from spreading yourself too thin.

McDonald's Restaurants are reputed worldwide for their hamburgers, pure and simple. That's their core product. Ray Kroc was a milkshake machine salesman and his clients were mainly fast-food restaurants. One day in the 1950's he stumbled onto the little drive-in restaurant in the American Midwest run by the McDonald brothers who were cooking hamburgers in an entirely different way: The assembly-line method of cooking. He had an idea and the result became the joint venture that today has literally revolutionized the entire fast-food industry.

Win the beginning; McDonald's had no more than 3 simple items on their menu: hamburgers, fries, and shakes. Up to this day and hopefully in the future, you will never find a hot dog at a McDonald's. However, today they have hamburgers in every food category possible. They offer hamburgers, cheeseburgers, chicken burgers, fish burgers, double burgers, rib burgers, and on and on. They have small fries, medium fries, large fries, and super-size fries. That's the power of core expansion.

Nevertheless, how does this apply to you? Let's say you are a computer programmer and you offer consulting work. You may provide initial consultations, research, programming, implementation, testing, hardware installation, training, customization, upgrades, licensing, and so on. Obviously, all of these elements may probably be part of one global package that relates to an area in which you are specialized. But by dividing your core into individual components, you may not have expanded in a direct sense but you have, however, expanded your possibilities.

Similarly, you may offer an entire package right now but fail to recognize that it's many different components – parts that can be individualized and offered separately.

Look at what you currently offer and write down every little detail that's part-and-parcel of what you offer. See if each part can be marketed separately. You can include this in your brochure.

Using the previous example, you could develop your own research division, program development division, implementation division, training division, and so on. The word "division" means exactly what it says. And by doing so, you may stumble onto clients who may need the entire package and others who may only need, say, a training specialist or a programmer. Keep in mind that you shouldn't digress from your specialization, but try to remain within your core and expand from within. While you may have narrowed your niche, through division, the demand for your products or services will likely increase even with prospects outside of your target market.

You can also add new products or services to your portfolio that stick to your niche. Look at dry-cleaners: They offer dry-cleaning, tie cleaning, tailoring, clothing storage and so on. If you do expand in such a way, don't just leave it at that. Put names on your new divisions that specifically describe the added portion of your business, or add a tagline to its name and/or description. As well, aside from dividing from within you could also divide your clientele into groups. While they may still be part of your niche, you have classified them into several categories that will naturally increase your hit ratio when approaching clients.

And finally, let's say that your package is simple and non-dividable. In almost every case I've encountered of this nature, there is still a portion that can be expanded by setting up strategic alliances with specialists in other fields (see Secret #10). For example, as a mortgage consultant your package involves helping people plan the most important purchase of their lives. However, when it comes to related services such as closing, you use a local closing agent (e.g. attorney or title company) with whom you've set up a strategic alliance. This provider gives a special price break offered exclusively to your specific clients as a way to create more business. The closing agent is glad to help since he or she knows that by doing so you will constantly send the closing agent more clients.

In your package, you can have a service called "Incredible Closing Incentive," which includes the scheduling, planning, closing and recording the legal documents. (Also, the survey, home inspection and appraisal could involve the co-services of other alliances, as well as the closing agent.) You see, you are not competing with the closing agent but both of you are seeking a same target market. We will deal with this further. But for now, remember that by dividing your core you will paradoxically multiply your chances of getting more business.

Take It Step-By-Step

A big mistake businesspeople often make is when they try to sell themselves as much as possible directly in every communication they produce. In the case of advertising, for instance, they try to draw up immediate clients through institutional advertising or what I call "advertising overkill." When meeting people for the first time, they blab on until the cows come home. When sending out information, they send packages that make shipping crates look like a joke!

They think that by selling themselves right in the ad they will get not only an immediate response but also immediate business. This oftentimes backfires and can even take away clients. Many clients I've dealt with usually get as a result of this type of approach a lot of calls but no business – or at least no long term business. They end up dealing with a lot of people who are merely curious but never serious. Because of hyper competition and the problem prospecting creates, trying to look for pre-qualified prospects can sometimes be worse than a needle in the haystack.

A new concept (although it's been around for years, but has recently become very popular) is direct-response marketing. It is a process in which businesses seek an immediate response as a result of their marketing efforts. While direct response marketing is often used to sell in the immediate sense, many use this technique to offer a free report, item, or service. Little do people know that the direct response strategy is usually not the true goal of the advertiser.

For instance, have you ever seen an infomercial by Charles Givens International? His commercial shows who he is and what he does, which is to help people make or save money, and then advertises a "free" seminar in the city in which the commercial is being televised. Now, do you think he's really doing this for free and traveling across the country only to educate people? In a sense, yes. But when people arrive at his seminar, they get tiny tidbits of information that will help them start to make or save money, but it's a certain kind of information that, if participants want to use it or want to have it continually updated, forces them to join the organization.

Mr. Givens' membership fees range in the hundreds and even thousands of dollars, and additional products (mostly information, books, reports, etc) are sold "in the back of the room" at his seminars. That's the power of pre-qualified lead generation! People who came out to see him are not general, curious, uninterested, and unqualified prospects. They have indirectly screened themselves. Once they show up, they are pre-qualified and highly targeted. And after they've been enticed with the free information, they are also pre-sold and ready to do business.

You see, people who may need your services may fit your demographics. But people who come forward without any selling efforts on your part, fit your psychographics. Psychographics are the portion of your demographics that not only need your services but also want what you have to offer.

In your case, if you offer a specific product or service that caters to a specific target market, find out ways to make your market come forward with minimal effort on your part. This is called "lead generation marketing". The best way to do this is to offer a free report of some kind. The report doesn't have to be product-specific, service-specific, industry-specific, or benefit-specific. It doesn't even have to directly relate to what you're selling. As long as it targets an audience that fits within your demographics (and eventually your psychographics), you're ahead of the game.

A used car salesperson once placed a small classified ad in the local newspaper that read something like this: "Is your car a lemon? Do you know that there are ways to turn your lemon into cash? Before you get rid of your clunker, call for my free report '10 Ways to Turn Your Lemon into Lemonade'!" In fact, he even used the pseudonym "The Lemon-Aid Institute."

And guess what? People who answered his ad were not only in the market for a new car, but they were also frustrated with their previous dealership for selling them their "lemon". They were enticed to seek more information from that specific dealership, that specific salesperson, and his specific inventory. In the end, not only were they pre-qualified but also they were positively impacted by the valuable "extra" service the salesperson provided. Car buyers therefore placed more confidence in that salesperson and also felt more comfortable in sending him referrals!

Let's say you're a financial planning consultant. You sell services such as investments, mutual funds, and savings plans. Rather than place an ad that directly markets these services, you could place a small classified ad promoting a free course, seminar, or report on helping people to save money. The idea is to have people come to you rather than you to them. Being in the information age, I personally prefer the "free report" style of lead generation. The incentive you offer doesn't have to relate directly to what you do. As long as it logically appeals to the same target market, you're on your way. If you recall from an example used earlier, you can turn your answering machine into a 24-hour salesperson for you. Your free offer should therefore be included in the message people hear – they must be invited to act somehow such as to receive the free report.

When it comes to advertising though, you shouldn't try to go into large circulation newspapers or general publications. I will deal with this issue in the next Secret, but remember for now that your main goal is not to create immediate clients. In general, the portion of the general public that fits into your product or service's demographics is merely made up of "suspects" (you suspect that they might need what you have to offer). When a portion of them comes forward to get your free report, sample, or service, you've isolated the true "prospects" from your suspects. Then, if they want more information or want more of what you've got, then they've become "expects" (you expect them to do business with you). This can be done in virtually all industries.

Here is an example of a salesperson for a music store specializing in pianos and keyboards. Older pianos usually require considerable repair since the wood inside holding the strings with which the piano creates its sound may be too old, cracking, and broken beyond repair. They constantly fall out of tune. The salesperson at the store had a small classified ad that said:

"Beware parents in the market for a piano!" (That was the headline.) "Many parents usually buy used pianos for their kids because they don't know if they'll love music and therefore want to minimize the risk of losing their investment. However, to the unsuspecting buyer, many used pianos are internally broken beyond repair and temporarily 'duped' in order to sound good and be sold quickly, only to become broken again when it's too late. Before you buy any piano, call for our free report 'Don't Let Piano Problems Put Your Bank Account Out of Tune: 6 Ways to Find Commonly Hidden Problems with Used Pianos'."

His report not only explained the possible faults commonly found in older pianos that can easily go unnoticed, but since he was catering to a specialized market (i.e., parents), his report went on to explain how used pianos fall out of tune quickly causing the child to learn the piano the wrong way and eventually to lose interest – let alone the parents money!

Of course, what the salesperson really wanted was to get these parents to buy new or professionally refurbished pianos from his store and especially from him. The resulting effect, however, was that the report not only brought prospects to his door but also instilled in them a greater confidence in the salesperson in addition to the reasons for buying a certified piano rather than a used one. Last time I heard, he made a fortune using this technique! Not surprised, are you?

In essence, look at lead generation advertising or multi-step marketing as a form of job search. People often send bulky résumés to potential employers in an attempt to sell themselves as much as possible, when very often their attempts get filed away -- into the "round" file, that is! Successful career consultants stress the importance of summarizing a résumé as much as possible, including past accomplishments and bottom-line results (instead of duties and responsibilities from previous jobs), and of putting it all on one single page. Why? Because, simply put, the résumé is not meant to land a job but to land an interview.

Lead generation should be regarded in the same way. The ad must be small, contain a concise message, stress an immediate benefit (something for free), and offer a useful tool or cause the prospect to want to know more. And this can be applied in virtually all fields and for many if not all types of products or services. What can you offer your prospects to arouse their curiosity and interest? What can you give away to entice them to get more? If you're giving something away, something that's somehow tied to what you do, you'll realize that what you're really doing is not giving away stuff but generating better leads. Nevertheless, keep in mind that the cost of giving away stuff can be far less than the cost of mass marketing!

Speak Softly (But Carry A Big Stick)

The following secret is probably the greatest secret in "Master Positioning." Now that we've talked about lead generation advertising, the next step is where to advertise. And the trick to having as many pre-qualified prospects come forward is to have your ad noticed and read by such a specific group of people as much, as often, and as effectively, as possible. General publications won't do that and they certainly cost a lot of money... That's cost-per-lead money.

Specialized publications, on the other hand, have the distinction of appealing to a specific audience and thus increase the chances of it being noticed as well as read. If one newspaper has a readership of 100,000 but only 25,000 of this number fits into your demographics, where another has a readership of only 40,000 but all of which fits into your demographics, which one do you think will give you the greatest response? In other words, rather than fishing for small fish in the middle of the ocean, you'll be a catching big fish in a small pond. Think of the specialized publication as sonar that will help you to find the specific kind of fish you really want.

This is not only due to the fact that the readership of a specialized publication will match your demographics but also the fact that people who buy these types of publications have a tendency to read them from cover to cover. Unlike a mass-published newspaper that will only be sifted through (i.e., it is bought by many but read in its entirety by few), a specialized publication will be read more intensely and thoroughly (i.e., it is bought by few but read in its entirety by many).

Your per capita hit-ratio will dramatically increase than if you would have advertised in a major publication that's too general or too vague. Your little ad can easily get "lost" in such large media or get drowned in a sea of ads. These days, specialized publications exist by the truckloads! Occupation-specific, special interest, or industry-specific publications can include newsletters, trade publications, journals, reports, corporate mail, magazines, specialty newspapers, catalogues, and communiqués from specific organizations and associations.

There are numerous publications for specific people or with specialized topics. For instance, if you go to your library, you will find that there are magazines for home-based businesses, newsletters exclusively written for corporate executives, magazines purely about cigars, newspapers strictly published for firemen, and even magazines geared for – of all things – gerbil breeders! As long as the readership logically fits into your target market and, if possible, into your psychographic criteria, this is where you will get the greatest bang for your marketing buck.

An advertising agent specializing in computer-based firms can advertise an offer for a free report in computer magazines or, better yet, in magazines read particularly by computer firms (such as hi-tech or Internet magazines). A medical consultant should advertise in medical journals, medical association newsletters, or medical equipment manufacturer catalogues – anywhere that puts him or her in front of as many doctors' eyeballs as possible. Anyway, you get the drift. The trick is to have your ad noticed and read by your target market as specifically as possible.

By the way, having your own newsletter is also a powerful way to attract prospects. If you haven't yet started one, get on it. Your newsletter may be offered for free or at a nominal cost to pay for the printing and distribution, but the idea is to have the people who read it want more and come forward to get it! As well, you can sell advertising space in your newsletter to, or swap ad space with, firms also catering to your unique clientele (again, this is what I call developing strategic alliances). Conversely, you can buy advertising space in a newsletter written by another firm that also caters to your specific target market. The possibilities here are endless.

However, it wouldn't be right for me to end this portion of this secret without discussing the Internet. With information being one the major shifts the world has experienced, the Internet can help to make your presence known in a better, quicker, and cheaper way. If you're not on the 'Net yet, you're losing out big time! But if you are, your Web site and email addresses, which should appear in all your business literature, should be made available to everyone with whom you come in contact, even as part of your signature on any other form of correspondence.

Email helps prospects to come forward in the privacy and convenience of their own homes or offices, and it also gives you a chance to respond to them immediately. It's truly a dynamic form of communication that, to this day, is still often overlooked. For example, with an email announcement list, discussion list, or electronic newsletter (often called "ezine"), you have the opportunity to remain in constant contact with your prospects and clients, develop credibility, and build relationships with them. So, invite people to subscribe in every communication you make. We'll talk more about this a little more later.

If you haven't already, create a homepage. Many people think this is expensive, which for a large sophisticated Web site can be, but a single Web page is far different than a Web site in that it's usually a part of a greater Web site – a chapter of a book, if you will. These sites are usually called domains. Many Internet providers have domains on which your Web page can be stored (many are actually free). While it may not be as sophisticated as having your own domain, it's a good start. Either way, it is a low cost way to be on the Web and it doesn't have to be slick with high-resolution graphics. The important thing is to maintain a presence on the Web.

Your page can be strictly information-oriented identical to a book or newsletter. Your homepage can be designed to advertise you, your company, and the products and services you offer. But most important, it can be a wonderful tool for people to access your free report. If your report is written in a two-dimensional printed format, more than likely you will have it on some diskette. Therefore, by having it available via the Internet, people can access your free information and print it themselves at home or at the office, without costing any money, time, or postage on your part.

However, don't make your free report available directly in your homepage. Many people who choose to use the multi-step marketing process I described earlier (which I strongly encourage) want the names and addresses of those people coming forward for future follow-up and direct mail possibilities. In this case, they have a special section of their web page that includes their free report, but it is one to which only people who have a password can access.

If you use this technique and people have seen your ad somewhere let alone your homepage in which you advertise your free report offer, they can write or email you to obtain their special, secret, free, and active-for-a-limited-time-only password. Once "inside," they can read your report and do so instantaneously.

They now have access to super-useful information and feel part of an elite group of educated members. Your printed newsletter can also be made available through password-protected access. If your newsletters carry a subscription cost, you can charge people in order for them to obtain their password and you can bill them regularly for renewal.

Remember that you're not trying to advertise with the hope of stumbling onto a trickle of suspects. You want an endless stream of pre-qualified, pre-screened, and pre-sold expects! As this secret states, you don't want to shout in order to attract prospects. You want to speak softly but carry a big stick with which you can lure better leads and "clobber 'em" (with your freebie, information, or expertise) when they're in proximity. For example, people who visit your site and read your Web page will hopefully want more. But even when only a small portion do, you know in advance that those who do are much more qualified, which saves you a lot of time and effort than trying to fish in a dried up desert of possible suspects.

In addition, once you're on the Web there are many more advantages that come with using this medium, such as search engines. Search engines are like electronic yellow pages that contain mostly every page and email address available on the Web. (However, there are specific ways to use search engines effectively, and we'll come back to this in later.) You can also link your page to other sites and get your link posted on those that also cater to your specific market (i.e. your real estate agents, builders, attorneys, etc.). This is simply another way to advertise through specialized means.

Nevertheless, it's all part of a lead generating system, and you know what "system" stands for, don't you? It stands for "Save Your Self Time, Effort, and Money!" Yeah, that's the ticket!

DAVID L. HANCOCK

Become A Celebrity

In the second secret, you learned that you should be the leader in your category or in your unique area of expertise. Now you need to be known as such. A friend of mine in Virginia has his own show on radio show – yes, his very own radio show! Radio, Cable and community television stations are wonderful mediums to get the word out effectively. This is an area in which you can get a lot of publicity at little or no cost (if you use your cooperative advertising secret).

This friend, a mortgage consultant of course, hosts a show called "The Debt Free Express" (sound familiar) on which he is either being interviewed or playing the role of the interviewer, with guests ranging from home owners looking for debt management solutions, to other consultants in areas similar to his own. He also takes calls on the show and has an email format where people can ask questions online and to which he'll answer directly on the air. The show is meant to advertise him directly – but perceived as a public service.

Publicity is greatly different than advertising. There are many different ways to get publicity out there, let alone free publicity. But the idea behind publicity is not to market your business or product (or at least not directly). Your goal through publicity is to get yourself known and known as an expert in your field. Publicity is far more credible than advertising. If you have narrowed your focus to a very specific, highly specialized field, publicity will come easy to you. The media loves to receive information from people who are uniquely qualified in their specialty.

Do you write articles for your local newspaper or write letters "to the editor"? Do you send out news releases to all the TV, newspaper, and radio stations in at least your area? Do you offer free seminars in conjunction with non-profit or not-for-profit organizations during, for instance, fundraisers? Do you offer to speak at luncheons, clubs, and organizations such as the Rotary? Do you offer free services to charities or sponsor community projects? The list goes on.

A laser vision correction doctor sent out press releases to all the Radio & TV stations and offered to perform a surgery live on the air as part of a medical documentary. One well-known radio station took the bait. With the patient's consent and during the operation, cameramen filmed the doctor performing the procedure and the radio reporter carried on detailed conversations and occasionally asked questions, such as: "What exactly are you doing now, Dr.?" The doctor replied by describing his actions. Not only did it cause his practice to get flooded with calls, but the doctor also had the bright idea to obtain the permission to mass-copy the event on videotapes and mail them as part of his information package to potential patients.

The show created a lot of "buzz" and the surgery was the talk of the town. I don't know if he actually did this, but if I were in his shoes, I would have the tape digitized and available to be played on the Internet. People accessing his Website can view the clip right in their own homes. Some people I know have their interviews, conferences, speeches, or voices digitized and plug it on the 'Net as well. Of course, everybody can do that. But if you're not on the Web, yet have a copy of a TV or radio interview/report on cassette, get the rights to it and send it to everyone who wants one, including potential referral-sources and strategic alliances.

A temporary help agency specializing in providing administrative support personnel to the public sector had a neat idea once. Their clients are mostly purchasing agents and, one year, a golf tournament was being held for – believe or not – government purchasing agents! (I believe it was to raise money for some charitable foundation.) The tournament was held in the middle of summer and it happened to be a hot day. So, the salesperson in the temporary help agency, wearing a T-shirt bearing the company logo and 1-800 phone number, rented a golf cart and loaded it up with coolers containing soft drinks. He drove his cart from hole to hole and offered free drinks to all the golfers in the tournament! In addition to the exposure this gave him, he was also given a chance to speak at the awards ceremony and mingle with the crowd as a result.

If you're an expert (and by specializing and narrowing your business, you are one) you must get out-and-about and make yourself known as one. For example, I know of an insurance agent who decided to specialize in life insurance for newlyweds and new families. His company didn't require it from him, but he decided on his own to develop an expertise in this particular area. You'll often find him at bridal fairs, bridal shows, home-buyers seminars, home furnishing stores, banks and mortgage-lending institutions, toy stores, baby clothing stores, and so on.

Now, for a typical insurance agent to do this kind of stuff may or may not be a waste of time. But how much more effective will he be if he promotes himself at those special events or locations as an insurance agent strictly catering to new couples and new families? Yep. Much more.

Do you have your free report written by now? If so, write a query letter to newspapers for an article you wish to contribute. A query letter is one in which you address the editor and propose a topic, on which you have an expertise, for an interesting article you would like to submit. Make sure that the headline of your query grabs their attention and makes them want to read it. Make your article somehow related to your free report. Give them a brief outline of your article along with a summary of your free report as a sort of "tickler." Don't forget to include in your query that you're not looking for any compensation (at least not for now), but ask if you can add a byline.

A byline is a small note at the end of your article describing the author and how he or she can be reached. Send the same query letter to as many newspapers as you can, especially specialized publications read by your target market. By the way, always ask for publishing rights so that the paper doesn't prevent you from having your article published elsewhere.

Now, write! Your article should not be promotional but may contain some highlights of your free report. Your byline can and should invite people to order it. It can say something like:
"David Hancock is the 'The Marketing Master', an author, speaker, and consultant specializing in business development and marketing communications. If you wish to learn more about the ideas written in this article, you can obtain a free copy of the complete report, 'Affiliate Cash Flow Marketing Handbook', at: www.AffiliateCashFlowMarketing.com."

Since your articles do not appear blatantly promotional, they help market your expertise far more effectively and carry far more weight than any self-serving advertisement. They grant you greater credibility because, like publicity (which is far more believable than advertising), they imply your superiority and your expertise rather than state it outright. And since implication is more powerful than specification, publicity will help solidify your leadership in the mind of the marketplace faster, more effectively, and for a longer period of time than any other form of promotion.

There's an old saying that goes: "Talk good about me or talk bad about me. But either way, please talk about me!" So, get out and about! Get others to know you and talk about you.

Seek Out & Spread Out

I know that the yellow pages' people will hate me for this, but your yellow pages' ad, although an essential part of your entire marketing machine, doesn't have to be of a large size, in color, prominently displayed, or tied-in with other gimmicks that the yellow pages salespeople have to offer. While necessary, the yellow pages should only be used as support systems.

The concept of this entire book is to teach you that creating top-of-mind positioning (not "institutional" advertising) should be your main marketing goal. When people have seen your ad, heard about you, or have a need for your services at any particular time, your contact information may or may not be available to them at that particular moment. Therefore, you want the yellow pages to back you up and not use them as a full-blown marketing medium.

Yellow pages salespeople more than likely don't have to sell you on the need to be in their directory, but where they make their commissions is by making your transaction as hefty as possible by selling you on size, color, and other gimmicks. Don't need it! Your presence is all that matters. However, there are some basic rules that you should follow.

First of all, the title of this secret is: "seek out (support systems) and spread out (among them)." Indeed, I'm a fervent believer in support systems since, when creating top-of-mind positioning, your potential clients may not necessarily need you and respond to you at that moment, but they may do so later when your contact information may not be available to them.

Whether it's local directories, specialty directories, occupation-specific registries, industry-specific directories, yellow pages, search engines, Internet directories, or trade publications, you should seek them out and list your company in as many of them as you can. The trick, however, is to spread out. Essentially, being there (and being everywhere) is what matters.

Don't be prominent in size or display. You can have a small black-and-white telephone ad carrying the name of your company, your tagline, your specialization, your "unique" product or service, and, if possible your free report offer. However, spreading out, especially within a single directory, is your best bet for a high visibility and hit-ratio. For example, if you're a mortgage consultant specializing in at-home applications, your ad can say: "Mary Lou of 'Home Loans on Wheels' – Your In-House Mortgage Consultant! Specializing in on-site loan application and the creator of 'Hassle-Free Mortgages'. To see how I can make sure that your loan as easy a watching TV, or for a free copy of my report 'Bringing Home Loans, Home', call..."

Now, here's the trick. The yellow pages people might tell you to be in only one particular location of their directory. Don't. Try to be in as many locations that logically relate to your firm or your service. Your ad can be small but it should appear in as many sections of the directory as possible. For instance, beyond the obvious "Mortgage" section of the directory, the previous ad can also appear in "Loans", "Real Estate", "Free Services", "Financial Planners", and even "Senior Citizen Services".

This also applies to the Internet, with search engines and directories like "Yahoo" and "Alta Vista." You should not only try to be on as many search engines as possible, but try to spread out as much as possible among them as well. For instance, a search engine is one in which you conduct a search based on a keyword – a word that you want the search engine to look for. It will search their entire database and find as many Web sites that contain your keyword.

You might register your homepage according to a specific set of keywords, but if you register it under numerous keywords your hit-ratio will increase dramatically. Keywords don't necessarily have to relate to your content. Those that also indirectly relate to your content – let alone to your firm, product, or service – should also be included. For instance, they should comprise of any word that may be tied to benefits you provide and the market you're targeting.

For example, a baker specializes in cookies. They not only bake many different kinds of cookies but also create different shapes, sizes, designs, and arrangements with them. One of their many creations are little cookie baskets with bows and lettering for, among other things, weddings, bridal showers, and baby showers. So, what did she do? She registered her page under the keywords "cookies", "weddings", "marriages", "showers", "baby", "brides", "grooms", "party", "cakes", "church", "gifts", "family", "souvenirs", "ideas", "shopping", and so on.

Another support system that is often ignored is the answering machine. Your answering machine should not be regarded as simply being a means of taking your calls and messages. Turn it into a support system as well. In fact, turn it into a salesperson working for you 24 hours a day, 7 days a week. Your message should invite people to do something. Does your message invite people to just leave a message? Or does it invite them to place an order for your free report?

Telephone companies usually offer multi-choice or multi-box phone services. This is when the caller has the ability to either leave a general voicemail message or press a number in order to leave a message for a specific recipient in another voice mailbox on the system. There's also the option to choose the number of boxes you wish to have available on your phone. However, a mailbox doesn't need to be associated with an actual person. Here's a sample message: "Hi! You've reached Bill White of 'Investment Mastery Inc.', where people learn how to be wise with their wealth. If you wish to leave me a message, press 1. To order my free report 'Money-Making Magic: 8 Sure-Fire Strategies for Making Money in Stocks', press 2..."

Ultimately, the object of "seek out and spread out" is to use as many support systems as possible. You want to be in front of your prospects when they have decided to buy or at least to hear what you've got. In other words, spread yourself out. Don't be big. Be everywhere!

DAVID L. HANCOCK

Make Your Net Work

Well, we've made it! You've now reached the last secret. And what better way to end this book that's jam packed full of marketing secrets other than by telling you about something I truly hate. I hate networking. Really, I do! I hate it because, in my experience, it hasn't brought me anything substantial in return. You're probably saying: "What? Has he lost his mind?"

But wait a minute; hear me out. Networking isn't a bad concept, far from it.

If the previous secrets have been properly followed, networking can be a fantastic marketing tool. If you can be at the top of your prospects' minds, you can also be at the top of your network's mind, right? Your special name, your tagline, your "unique" product or service, your free reports, your lead generators, your celebrity status, and your support systems, all added to your network of referral-sources, can and should bring you an incredible amount of business.

However, here's the problem. Having a network and having a networking system are two entirely separate things. When you're only networking, more often than not people will want something in return or else they will either stop sending you clients or simply lose interest (if you don't take the time to recognize their efforts, and that's if you have any time left at all). So, how can you reward your network? Better yet, how can you turn your network into a networking system? The answer is by developing and establishing a network of strategic alliances.

All throughout this book you have read about techniques in setting up strategic alliances in some form or another. They were included in the many examples you've read up to now. Essentially, there are as many different forms of systematized networking opportunities out there as there are businesses, and I strongly encourage you to vigorously seek them out. But in my experience, I have found that they mainly fall into three major categories. The first is what I call the info-network, the second the auto-network, and the third the intra-network. Let's take a look at each of these systems and how you can apply them to your situation.

Info-Networking

The information-based network is one in which a strategic marketing alliance is created also known as a "Joint Venture". This alliance is one in which information is exchanged in some form or between parties. Basically, that information includes qualified leads that both you and your alliance share, or information about each other that is promoted to each party's market (also known as "cross-promotion"). As long as your strategic alliance logically shares a same target market without directly competing with you, there is an immense potential there for you to consider.

For instance, I mentioned to you earlier about the power behind the free report and especially the newsletter. Advertising space can be sold at a nominal cost in order to pay for the printing and distribution of your newsletter, or it can be offered to those that might be happily interested in being directly promoted to your market. In turn, you should seek out advertising spaces in newsletters, brochures, corporate literature, or catalogues of potentially mutually beneficial alliances. The obvious advantage is that it can save you and them money by swapping ads.

This also refers to mailing lists where you can swap each other's prospect or client lists. Mailing lists seem to have increased in popularity these days and, if used properly, can produce good results.

Mailing list brokers sell or lease mailing lists that you can use to conduct direct mail and telemarketing campaigns – lists of people that match your specific demographics.

However, beware. Brokered mailing lists will be limited to only the demographic data you specify and not the psychographic element of your target market – that's impossible to discern, unless you or the brokers were psychics! Also, electronic mailing lists are a little more complicated. Email is a more intimate medium and privacy is becoming an increasingly important issue these days. Therefore, if you choose to use a broker's list for your direct email campaign, make sure to choose a reputable and ethical firm where you are guaranteed that subscribers have voluntarily submitted their email addresses. Such lists are often called "opt-in".

In order to curtail both these problems, a better solution is to seek out strategic alliances and ask, rent, or buy their list of prospects and clients. Most of them will approve especially when you trade your list of clients or prospects with them. But if you have to rent or buy their lists, the cost will definitely be far less than that of one coming from a broker – they're not cheap!

Most strategic alliances are not accustomed to the idea of sharing their lists and will therefore be happy with just a few bucks. The added advantage, however, is that since you know from where these lists originate you will have a much better handle on the quality (the psychographic element) of the recipients. And as far as email and privacy are concerned, info-networking doesn't mean that there has to be an actual mailing list exchange. You can swap ezine ads, single mailing announcements or exclusive special offers endorsed by each list owner.

Nevertheless, should you decide to use targeted mailing lists to market your free report offer, it should yield you a substantially greater result than ordinary, unsolicited, general public mailings. For instance, direct mail directed to the public usually result in a mere 1 to 5% response, while direct mail to a predetermined demographic would likely produce an 8 to 13% response. However, if your free report is used in your campaign, and if your goal is only to generate pre-qualified leads and not immediate sales or clients, your chances of beating the 25% mark will be easy.

Auto-Networking

Auto-networking is the process of creating referral-sources that automatically supply you with good quality leads, without you having to lift a finger. Brochure stands, posters, flyers, coupons, and business cards can be set up at the offices of potential referral-sources. Again, I hate networking, especially when I have to work for them (or, in other words, nurture them). So, auto-networking doesn't mean to give out cards or literature to a possible referral-source and then hoping it will produce something in return. It means setting up a system between both of you where, since you are catering to a same market, you have made an arrangement (in writing, if possible) to constantly supply each other with materials and information.

An example is a dry-cleaner who discovered that the largest clientele of a busy restaurant near its location was mostly made up of executives having "power lunches" (those business lunches the tax people love to hate). The dry-cleaner, knowing that her greatest clientele is also made up of executives who bring their shirts or dresses to have cleaned, saw it as an opportunity.

Coupons were made and handed out by the restaurant's waiters and waitresses along with their clients' food tabs. They offered a 5% discount on dry cleaning services and the coupons could be accumulated up to a maximum of 25% – of course they were valid for a limited time only. In return, the dry-cleaner handed out coupons (clipped to the garment bags of their clients' dry-cleaning) offering a free appetizer or dessert at that particular restaurant – good for one per person per lunch – with every incoming order of $30 worth of dry-cleaning.

But it didn't stop there. They exchanged posters, flyers, coupons, and printed materials (such as the restaurant's menu and the dry-cleaner's brochure). They marketed it all under the banner of "Don't let the spot on your shirt from the juiciest roast beef in town at Jenny's Restaurant ruin that big deal! Bring it to Sparkling Cleaners, the first dry-cleaner for the busy executive, because 'Power Lunches Deserve a Clean Image'. With Jenny's Restaurant and Sparkling Cleaners, you can take your clients to lunch and take a bite out of dirt!"

By the way, I must take a moment to ask you a question. In the previous example, particularly in the marketing approach the dry-cleaner and restaurant took, were included some of my other Secrets. Can you guess what they are? The obvious ones are hard to miss. They carried the trademark symbols, indicated that they specialized in one area, and had taglines added to their names.

But the one that might have gone unnoticed is the category in which the dry-cleaner placed its business. Being the first dry-cleaner specializing in executive dry-cleaning is probably a little misleading and most likely untrue, but by calling itself the first dry-cleaner for the "busy" executive, it has created its own unique category. (All right, all right. I was just checking!)

Another form of auto-networking is, as the saying goes, "You can't teach an old dog new tricks", but you can surely teach a new dog to cook you breakfast! Creating networking systems with potential referral-sources who are either approached by competitors or already implicated in other secrets may be difficult. So, what can you do? You get them while they're starting out.

Previously, I showed you how important it is for you to get known in your market or industry as the expert, the celebrity in your field. By conducting speeches, sponsorships, seminars, and the like, you are creating that all-important top-of-mind positioning. Many of the members in your audience should encompass potential referral-sources. But referral-sources have to come from somewhere, don't they? So, if you can approach them before they are about to become potential targets for your competitors, you can save yourself a lot of effort and grief.

For example, I coach mortgage consultants to get themselves known among the community and possibly set up strategic alliances with them by, among other things, setting up cooperative brochures or flyers to use within the real estate community. However, if they've been in the industry for a while, many of these consultants may have already been approached by other consultants or may have a fixed idea in their minds of which consultant to whom they would refer their clients for their lending needs. In that case, we just try to set ourselves apart from the pact (I'll expand in a minute, I promise).

In my consulting work, I help mortgage consultants to set up special presentations as "guest lecturers" at local attorney or escrow offices and real estate schools. Schools love it, since its part of their curriculum to teach future real estate professionals on the mechanics of mortgage lending. Some courses also make it an essential part of their licensing preparation requirements. By giving a lecture or presentation, the mortgage consultant not only gets his name inculcated into the minds of these future real estate professionals, but he has also created an almost impenetrable barrier against competitors wanting a "piece-of-the-pie." By being part of their schooling, they naturally became a part of their minds! After all I don't recommend a newbie to take on the top real estate agent in the marketplace, they'd be slaughtered. Start with the next generation and help them help you!

This technique can be applied in almost every industry, with trade schools, business schools, community colleges, government services, unemployment insurance subsidized courses, and so on. A government software programmer can give a small computer presentation during courses that the government provides to recently hired purchasing agents. A wedding planner can give small courses during pre-nuptial classes (also know as "marriage preparation"). An accountant specializing in corporate taxation can give small seminars to young entrepreneur workshops (most chambers of commerce offer this type of service). And the list goes on.

Intra-Networking

Think of intra-corporate divisions, Intranets, and intrapreneurs (employees owning a portion of their employer's company). Intra-anything simply means two or more parts of a whole that are independent but at the same time inter-dependent. Basically, this is the old bartering system that goes back centuries. But in the context of intra-networking, however, it is not a direct exchange of product for product or service for service (even product for service), but an exchange of a service or product for information, clients, referrals, or promotional efforts.

For instance, a car wash owner makes an arrangement with a local gas station to offer coupons to each client that comes to pump gas. They were given the permission to hang posters in the station, leave menus at the counter, and place signs on the pumps. In return, for every 10 coupons the car wash received, the employees at the station were given a free car wash. It later developed to promoting each other.

A freelance writer edits corporate newsletters and targets her market as well. She will then have her articles and personal advertisements published for free in the newsletter in exchange for editing their business correspondence, and the newsletter itself. Hotels make up the majority of the clientele of an advertising agent specializing in elevator advertising. Hotels place the agent's brochures in rooms and executive suites for free in exchange for free advertising space in the elevators of other businesses and office buildings.

What kind of product or service do you offer from which a potential (and potentially effective) referral-source may benefit? Think of ways of being able to offer your products or services for free in exchange for pre-qualified leads or, as mentioned in info-networking, promotional efforts. Intra-networking can also become powerfully effective if you were lucky enough to stumble onto another company that offers products or services that complement your products or services well, while at the same time sharing costs (such as advertising costs), leads, as well as clients.

Take the example of the mortgage consultant and the closing agent mentioned earlier. Now, the closing agent gives a special price break for your clients knowing that you will refer them to him. Obviously, this might relate more closely to the auto-networking style. But if the closing agent agrees to display your promotional materials, your business cards, your brochures, or your letterhead for free in exchange for a certain number of your clients, that's intra-networking at work!

Altogether, info-networking, auto-networking, and intra-networking are powerful tools to help make you create good referral-sources that work and never stop working. The idea is nonetheless to network but to do so wisely so as to be able to create as many leads and clients as possible with the least amount of effort. Don't network. Make your net work for you!

DAVID L. HANCOCK

Put It In Writing

Here's a bonus secret. And it is indeed a bonus since, with all that you have learned up to now, you would never be as effective if I didn't give this extra piece of advice.

I can never stress enough, whether it's in this book, in my day to day consulting work, or in my ezines that in order to create endless streams of new, repeat, and referral business, you must turn every single nook-and-cranny of your business into an effective marketing system. Every step you take during the normal course of your business activities should include making yourself known as the king or queen in your field – or at least in the minds of those who are in it. Therefore, all forms of correspondence, literature, promotional materials, advertising, and so on must contain at least 8 or 9 of these secrets – although all 10 would be much more effective.

The power of the written word has been proven scientifically, time and time again, to be of immense proportions. Roger Dawson, in his book "The Secrets of Power Negotiating: How to Get Anything You Want", emphasized a universal law, which states that people will believe more what they see in writing than what they don't. As Roger points out: "If it is said, it could be true. But if it is written, then it must be true." When positioning yourself in the mind of the marketplace, your efforts will be far more effective if they are done through the written word.

For example, writing your own book is indeed a tremendously effective if not essential tool for establishing your credibility. They say that you must "publish or perish." Today, that statement has greater meaning. In a society where people are bombarded with marketing messages and leery of claims of any kind, communicating your uniqueness, your competitive advantage, and your expertise through the written word (as with books, articles, endorsements, reviews, and media publicity) is far more credible and believable than any direct promotional message.

Nevertheless, start by putting things down in writing. If you don't have a brochure or publicity kit already made up, make one! If your fees are not listed on a fee schedule for all your clients to see, print one! If articles written by or about you have been published, make copies and pass them around! If you have reference letters especially written by clients who initially had concerns or objections, offer copies to prospects who have the same concerns! If you don't yet have a catalogue of your products or services (both in a packaged form and in divisions), create one!

I may be overly emphasizing the importance of putting things down in writing, but I feel that I can never stress it enough. Realize that the above items, along with all of the tools that you've learned in the ten previous secrets, are crucially important to have in writing in some form or another in order to create lasting top-of-mind positioning.

Let's take the example of the cosmetic surgeon one more time. A patient being consulted for surgery has concerns about pain. Now, if the doctor says that the procedure is painless, he will be somewhat believable. But how much more believable will it be if the doctor pulled out of a binder a testimonial written by a patient, one who had the same concern prior to his surgery, and in it claimed that the procedure was indeed painless? You guessed it. Lots more.

Finally, a quick word about written materials. Some years ago, I came across an article (I believe it was in "Entrepreneur Magazine") that gave statistics gathered from a recent survey conducted by a direct-mail marketing firm for a credit card company. The survey found the following results: Documents that are high in contrast (print versus paper) have pulled a greater response over colored print on colored paper. Traditional white on black is best, yet color on white or black print on light colored paper is just as good. Remember that, as long as you maintain a contrast between your text, graphics, pictures, and the paper you print them on, you're rolling.

The research also showed that borders around texts have also increased readership by 20% over plain text with faint or non-existent borders. It also found that certain words pulled more than others. These words include "save", "free", and "discover". Try using these words in your printed materials as much as possible. (By the way, it is my guess that one of these three words became the name of that credit card company conducting the research!) And more important, make sure they all contain (if not highly stress) your name, tagline, specialization, and unique category.

Michel Fortin is an internationally acclaimed and highly sought-after consultant whose marketing advice has helped countless clients earn millions of dollars in record time. He is also the Senior Editor of Internet Marketing Chronicles, a weekly newsletter with 125,000 subscribers, as well as the author of four books. His latest book, "Power Positioning Dot Com" reveals how to keep your product or service indelibly carved into your prospects' uppermost consciousness at all times. Click here for immediate access: www.davidlhancock.com/powerpositioning.

Close the Closing

Now we are going to get specific, mortgage specific. Sit back relax, grab your Mountain Dew™ and open your mind. No I'm not going to fill it with off the wall concepts or vague ideas just as an add-on; I'm going to give you instructions that you can measurably see results right now! Hang On!

Close the Closing
What? Stay with me here. Close the Closing means just that. If you are not already attending each and every closing you

are loosing 70% of your earned referrals! No kidding, 70%!

You've already invested in the client, gotten to know them and hopefully built a rapport with them; why not see them through! Most mortgage consultants are afraid to go in case something comes up, or because the process had some bumps in it.

HELLO! That is why YOU need to be there! Would you like to have an uninformed closing agent (or worse yet a hostile agent) talk a little too much. Here is an example: Let's say my client had a less than perfect credit history. So their rate was slightly higher than market. Not too far fetched, but higher. And of course less than perfect credit history usually means slightly higher fees as well.

My client wanted to select their own attorney, so we lost a little control there. When the attorney opened the package to start the closing his first words were "Look at this, this rate it is higher than market right now, and why are you being charged these fees…" I kid you not!

Fortunately, after building a rock solid foundation with the client, they spoke up and defended the loan for me (rare). They indicated that they knew what they were getting and why their situation deemed it necessary, and that I had committed to staying in contact with them by periodically reviewing their situation in hopes to improve the situation as soon as possible (there is another bonus secret there).

Go to every closing that is physically possible. No one else seems to be doing this, or at least very few. So few in fact that when you do show up, everyone either acts surprised or goes on about how special the client is that the lender came to see it through.

Now I hope your mouth is watering, because you will be able to look back in time and see the very day you started doing this, because your client will appreciate it and tell others. The attorney or closing agent will see and eventually appreciate you being there that they will refer clients to you. And so on...

Can you imagine taking a new direction where you actually refer clients to your real estate agents? Or better yet, refer new clients to real estate agents that you want to become part of you network!

Market the Flip Side
GROW YOUR BUSINESS AND
EXPLODE YOUR SALES

If you're committed to your success, this book filled with tips, strategies, tools and concepts will definitely be an asset for you and your business. But if you truly want to take your business to the next level listen to this. Oh, by the way, I hope you are still sitting down, because this is even more powerful, more "why didn't I think of that" than Closing the Closing!

Market the Flip Side

That's right! Market the Flip Side! You've already spent time and money with the current client and agent; why not realize triple the response on that effort?

This is part of my "Stealth Marketing Report" but here is basically what you need to do: Most real estate purchase transactions, the core of your business, have agents and sellers, correct. Those interested parties to your transaction need to know who you are! Remember earlier secrets to be unique? Well, day one on your next purchase transaction starts with marketing the flip side.

Now don't make the mistake of trying to sell the other agent or the sellers. Be stealthy; make them want to do business with you because they have to. Because they want to have the superior lender support like you are giving the buyer.

Contact the seller and listing agent via letter or phone call to introduce yourself and let them know you will be keeping them informed with the progress. Open the doors of communication, invite questions keep them up to date. This way you remain in control of the transaction and impress everyone involved.

You will eventually need to hire an assistant because your business will be growing exponentially. That same mortgage guru I mentioned earlier has a saying "If you don't have an assistant, you are one". So true.

DAVID L. HANCOCK

The Email Revolution

If you are not prepared, the next revolution that is right around the corner will leave you behind. It will be email. You need the ability to communicate directly to your prospects (just because you've closed the sale doesn't mean they are no longer prospects) via email, phone and physical address. This all needs to be managed so you to continuously communicate primarily with email.

Now, you need to know what works in the process of sending them email and building the content of your Autoresponder (I'll explain in a moment). That is what the rest of this book covers. Keep in mind, that all of us have the ability to write letters. It is just a matter of putting yourself to work and making it happen. Also keep this in mind as you read this book, "Do the uncomfortable until it becomes comfortable" and remember poverty comes at a great price. Make fear your partner, and put your life into an adventure; an adventure that will wrap itself around you and the rest of your life. Imagine where all of this may lead you. Are you ready for an adventure?

OK I didn't invent the Autoresponder, but I should have!

Autoresponders are cool. Email autoresponders work like a fax-on-demand system. Maybe you've seen systems where you call from your fax machine and dial a certain code and you'll get back a document in your fax machine? Well, an email autoresponder works the same way. If you send an email to an autoresponder address or add an email address to your list they'll get back a prewritten message.

Using a Sequential Email Autoresponder

Until just recently, you could only do a one-time autoresponder with one message coming back. But now you can set up a whole sequence of autoresponder messages going out on any day you choose. You see, I should have invented it, because it's so perfect for what we do. But I didn't. But we still love them!

For example, message number one might go out immediately, then message number two goes out two days afterwards, next message number three goes out on day five, then on day eight comes another message, etc, etc.

Do you see the real beauty of this whole thing? It's unbelievable. And the best part is everything is done automatically for you because it's triggered when a prospect submits their email address or you enter them into your system. So that means you can simply set up your system once and then it keeps working over and over again like a tireless machine making sure no prospect ever slips through the cracks. A sequential email autoresponder really turbo charges your follow-up efforts.

Here are a few important facts to consider and why sequential autoresponders can help counter these:

A recent study conducted by Sales and Marketing Executives International concluded that 81% of major sales are closed after the fifth contact. 80% of people who inquire about a product or service will buy it within one year of their initial inquiry. However, more than 90% of the time, they don't buy from the same company that they made their initial contact with.

I've reprinted (with permission) an excellent article by Michel Fortin explaining the importance of using sequential autoresponders:

How to be Sequentially Superior
Email is certainly an important aspect of marketing on (and off) the web. But a single email is never enough – and in fact can be more costly down the road. Like all marketing messages, it takes repetition in order to get people to first absorb the message, understand it and then take action. Naturally, some people will immediately

respond while others need to see the message more than once before they even think about responding to the offer.

The reason for this is that each person, with each marketing message and for each different type of product, has a specific responsive behavior. Virtually all markets can be divided into several, graduated segments based on such behaviors. They generally consist of five, which are: 1) Innovators, 2) early adopters, 3) early majority, 4) late majority and 5) laggards.

Innovators are risk-takers and venturesome, and consist of about 2.5% of the whole market. They usually respond to new offers almost immediately and without giving them much thought. On the other hand, early adopters respond to new ideas early – taking action soon after the innovators do, albeit carefully. They represent 13.5% of the market. While the third and fourth groups (i.e., the middle majority) constitute the largest segment, the early majority specifically typically respond to new ideas before the average person does. The early majority represent 34% of any given market. The late majority, which consists of another 34%, are skeptical, careful and slow. They take their time, usually shop around and need to see offers more than a few times before giving them any consideration. The final segments (or the laggards) take action only after some time has elapsed – usually after everyone else has done so. They consist of the remaining 16% of the entire pie.

Ultimately, the important thing to note here is that the middle majority altogether consist of a whopping 68%. A marketer's goal is therefore to effectively reach, persuade and incite this larger segment, which is often difficult to do with a single mailing. Repeating your marketing message – and sometimes doing so more than once – is essential with this group.

In the end, you will not only increase the response but also multiply it.

One ... Two ... Three Steps, you're In!

As you likely know, statistics prove that the bulk of most sales occur in the follow-up process. However, following up with your prospects is more than just a process – it's an art. You need to do so in a timely, consistent and compelling manner. You don't have to constantly sell; you could offer free information or relevant articles.

With the help of the Internet, campaigns can also be entirely automated with what are often called "follow-up" or "intelligent" autoresponders (or "autobots"). After someone has responded to your offer or asked for more information from your company, autobots can automatically deliver your series of pre-written follow-up email messages in preset intervals for ever if you want. This strategy can become quite effective, provided that users are properly notified – they are subscribing in other words – and given the ability to stop the flow at any time.

Another great strategy is to use smart autoresponders for delivering a series of informative articles over a period of time, which can be offered freely or even marketed as entirely separate, stand-alone products – such as a course or a reminder service. Nevertheless, there are many providers of these types of automated, sequential email systems.

In the beginning, I used to store my prospects' emails in a database and manually deliver regular mailings to them. That did the job but I was losing out on a much greater potential.

I wasted time and money doing all the follow-ups by hand, worked tirelessly to keep track of which prospect needed which message, and lost tons of sales when I stopped... I was leaving money on the table!

So, I decided to get a smart autoresponders that quite literally revolutionized the way I conducted my online marketing.

It helped put my marketing and follow-up almost completely on autopilot. What a difference! My sales shot up, my free time blossomed and my profits exploded!

Not only can you send broadcasts to people on your list; you can personalize your emails. You can include good for limited time offers and many other incredible benefits.

It took me a while before I understood the power of following up with my prospects. You too may not fully appreciate the benefits of using smart autoresponders in your business until you actually try them. I guarantee you'll be amazed!

Once you're up and running, and if you do it right, you'll start seeing the immense power of this tool almost immediately as it helps you convert up to 400% more prospects into future sales!

The best autoresponder service is GetResponse (www.davidlhancock.com/getresponse) and it's free.

DAVID L. HANCOCK

3 Killer Secrets for Closing the Sale

"Inherently, each one of us has the substance within to achieve whatever our goals and dreams define. What is missing from each of us is the training, education, knowledge and insight to utilize what we already have." -- Mark Twain

FACT: Selling is the only profession wherein your potential earnings are beyond what 95% of the world's population could ever earn – but only if you know how to close the sale. Selling is a wonderful profession – but because it is oftentimes difficult to become successful at it, it is also considered one of the toughest professions in the world.

As a salesperson, you need to be thankful that making the sale is so difficult, because if it were easy, the field would be flooded with amateurs – and the amount of money you could earn would be greatly reduced. Your job is to find ways to make the sales process easier so that you can become one of the highest paid people in your field, if not the world.

The Major Challenge in Selling

Closing the sale is perhaps the most stressful and challenging part of the sales process. This is where the rubber meets the proverbial road.

Brian Tracy says there are secrets I know that can unlock the real firepower that lies dormant in your very own selling skills, and these secrets will change the course of your sales career forever. I'm going to reveal 3 closing secrets that can easily triple your sales in the next 90 days.

You may have heard about his high-powered sales seminars attended by approximately 400,000 men and women each year in 23 countries - or perhaps you have come across one of his 16 best-selling books or 300 learning programs.

The 3 killer secrets that I'm about to reveal are excerpts of techniques he has taught to salespeople all over the world, many of whom have gone on to become the biggest money-makers in the sales industry. I guarantee that if you master these lessons and practice them faithfully, you will at least triple your sales within the next 90 days.

Killer Closing Secret #1: The Preference Close

The first technique is the Alternative Close – also called the Preference Close. It is based on the fact that people like to have choices. They don't like to be given what may sound like an ultimatum to either buy it or not buy it.

To apply this technique, you simply structure your close by saying, "Which of these would you prefer, A or B?"

With the alternative close, whichever one the customer selects, you would have made a sale either way. You should always try to give the customer two choices. Even if you are selling a single product, you can give him two choices with regard to payment, or delivery. For example, "Would you like this delivered to your office or to your home address?" "Will that be MasterCard or Visa?" "Would you like the ATM 26 or the ATM 30?" And so on.

Killer Closing Secret #2: The Secondary Close

The second closing technique is the Secondary Close. This is extremely popular. It is a way of helping a customer make a big decision by having him make a small decision that infers the big decision. Instead of asking the customer to go ahead with the product or service, you ask a question about a peripheral detail, the acceptance of which means that he has decided to buy the larger product.

For example, you could ask, "Would you want this shipped in a wooden crate, or would cardboard be all right?" "Would you like us to include the drapes and rods in the offer?" "Did you want the standard rims or would you like the customized racing rims on your car?"

In each case, if the customer agrees to or chooses the smaller item, he has indirectly said, "yes" to the entire offering. People often find it easier to agree to small details than they do to making a larger commitment. That's why this is sometimes called the Incremental Close, where you get commitment bit by bit to the entire offer.

Killer Closing Secret #3: The Authorization Close

The third closing technique is the Authorization Close, which is often used to conclude multimillion-dollar transactions. At the end of the sales conversation, the salesperson simply asks if the prospect has any questions or concerns that haven't been covered. If the prospect has no further questions or concerns, the salesperson takes out the contract, opens it up to the signature page, places a check mark where the customer has to sign, and pushes it over to him saying, "Well then, if you will just authorize this, we'll get started on it right away." The word "authorize" is better than the word "sign." A check mark is better than an X. Offering to "get started right away" is better than sitting there hoping for the best.

However you do it, be prepared to ask for the order in whichever ways seem appropriate at the moment.

Brian Tracy is a million-dollar master of peak sales performance and personal success strategies. As the world-renowned creator of 300 video and audio learning programs, and the best-selling author of 16 books, his ideas and approaches are used by most of the big money makers and the superstars of selling. In his RealVideo course, "24 Techniques for Closing the Sale," Brian shows you powerful tactics that can double or triple your sales closing rate – and teach you how to sell 50% to 100% of all prospects that you come in contact with - all in just 63 minutes.
www.davidlhancock.com/questions

The Triggers of Success:

How to Trigger a Successful Sale
through the Power of Psychological Triggers

A desire to buy something often
involves a subconscious decision. In fact, I
claim that 95% of buying decisions are
indeed subconscious.

Knowing the subconscious reasons
why people buy, and using this information
in a fair and constructive way, will trigger
greater sales response – often far beyond
what you could imagine.

I recall a time when I applied one of these subconscious devices by changing just one word of an ad, and response doubled. I refer to these subconscious devices as psychological "triggers." A psychological trigger is the strongest motivational factor any salesperson can use to evoke a sale.

There are 30 triggers in all, some of which I will reveal to you in a moment. Each trigger, when deployed, has the power to increase sales and response beyond what you would normally expect.

There are triggers, for example, that will cause your prospect to feel guilty if they don't purchase your product. Let me give you an example. Whenever you receive in the mail a sales solicitation with free personalized address stickers, you often feel guilty if you use the stickers and don't send something back – often far in excess of the value of the stickers. Fundraising companies use this method a great deal. You receive 50 cents worth of stickers and send back a $20 bill.

Another example is those surveys that are sent out asking for you to spend about 20 minutes of your time filling them out. Enclosed in the mailing you might find a dollar bill included to encourage you to feel guilty, and entice you to fill out the survey. And you often spend a lot more than one dollar of your time to do that.

Guilt is a strong motivator. I have to admit that I've used guilt in many selling situations – with great success, I might add.

I call one of the most powerful triggers a "satisfaction conviction," which is a guarantee of satisfaction. But don't confuse this with the typical trial period you find in mail order, i.e., "If you're not happy within 30 days, you can return your purchase for a full refund." A satisfaction conviction is different. Basically it takes the trial period and adds something that makes it go well beyond the trial period.

For example, if I were offering a subscription, instead of saying, "If at anytime you're not happy with your subscription, we'll refund your unused portion," and instead said, "If at any time you're not happy with your subscription, let us know and we'll refund your entire subscription price – even if you decide to cancel just before the last issue."

Basically you're saying to your prospect that you are so sure that they'll like the subscription that you are willing to go beyond what is traditionally offered with other subscriptions.

This in fact gives the reader the sense that the company really knows it has a winning product and solidly stands behind the product and your satisfaction.

Is this technique effective? You bet. In many tests, I've doubled response – sometimes by adding just one sentence that conveys a good satisfaction conviction.

I received an e-mail from a company requesting my advice. They had an e-mail solicitation that wasn't drawing the response that they had expected. What was wrong?

Looking over what they had created, I saw several mistakes, many of which would have been avoided if they knew the psychological triggers that cause people to buy. Let me give you just one example.

In the subject line of most e-mails that have solicited me, I have been able to tell, at a glance, that the solicitation was for a specific service or an offer of something that I was clearly able to determine. Examples such as "Reduce your CD and DVD costs 50%," Or "Lose weight quickly," pretty much told me what they were selling. Was this good or bad?

The problem with those subject lines is that the reader was able to quickly determine: 1) that it was an advertisement; and 2) that it was for some specific product or service.

Most people don't like advertising. And most people won't make the effort to open their e-mail solicitation if they think they are getting an advertising message – unless they are sincerely interested in buying something that the advertisement offers.

The subject line of an e-mail is similar to the headline of a mail order ad, or the copy on an envelope, or the first few minutes of an infomercial. You've got to grab somebody's attention and then get them to take the next step. In the case of the envelope, you want them to open it. In the case of an infomercial, you want them to keep watching, and in the case of an e-mail, you want them open up the e-mail and read your message.

The key, therefore, is to get a person to want to open your message by putting something into the subject area of your e-mail that does not appear to be an advertising message – one that would compel them to take the next step. And the best trigger to use for this is the trigger of curiosity.

There are a number of ways you can use curiosity to literally force a person to take the next step. You can then use this valuable tool to put a reader in the correct frame of mind to buy what you have to offer.

Once again, all the principles apply to every form of communication – whether it is advertising, marketing or personal selling. And to know these triggers is the key to more effective communication and most importantly, the avoidance of costly errors that waste time and money.

Joe Sugarman, the best-selling author and top copywriter who has achieved legendary fame in direct marketing, is best known for his highly successful mail-order catalog company, JS&A, and his hit product, BluBlocker Sunglasses. Joe's new breakthrough book, "Triggers," cracks the human psychological code by identifying 30 triggers that influence people to buy. Learn more at: www.davidlhancock.com/triggers

DAVID L. HANCOCK

Turn Everything You Say into Wealth, Well-Being & Personal Success

You might think this strange, but every day, before I start work, I stand up, look to the sky, throw my hands in the air, and shout out loud: "I feel terrific!"

This is what I call an 'affirmation' – positive self-talk to charge up my emotions and help me produce my very best work. An affirmation can be as simply as "YES!"... as uplifting as "I'm very happy at this moment!"... or as determined as "I'm willing to do whatever is necessary to succeed!"

Try it for yourself right now. Choose a positive message you want to tell yourself. Then stand up, put your head back, throw your arms up, and shout it out loud. Makes you feel uncomfortable? Good! You've just discovered how powerful words can be.

Unlimited Success & Wealth are All In the Words You Use.

What's the single most important asset you and your business possess? Forget money and numbers. The true currency of business is WORDS. Communicating your ideas, your offer, the benefits of your product – using words to achieve your aims is the single most important activity any business ever performs.

Unlimited success and wealth are as simple as using the right words. You can get everything you've ever wanted in life, simply by saying the right words – because the words which you communicate determine the quality of your life.

This is true whether communicating with others or with yourself. Especially with yourself.

Words have the power to induce someone to laugh, to cry, to be kind, to be loving, to be cooperative, or to buy. Or be unkind, angry, irrational.

Whether words are written or spoken, they have enormous power.

Of course, when words are spoken, the added factors of voice timbre, emphasis, emotion...all have the potential to cause even more impact.

Use Words to Achieve a Win-Win Situation.
Here is what few businesspeople seem to realize: People all over the world really want to help and accommodate their fellow humans. But they must be approached properly. The magic words I'll reveal to you in a moment can manipulate a situation to bring you what you want – which isn't necessarily a bad thing.

Magic Words Can Bring You Riches.

The same words, strategies and techniques that I've used to get the best results from everyday situation – like hiring a BMW for the price of a Ford, slashing the cost of a first class hotel room, and buying valuable antiques at huge discounts – can work magic for your business, too. Here are 3 of the phrases, which have helped me build a career marketing over $500,000,000 of both my own and my client's products and services.

Magic Phrase #1 – Attract All the Money You Need for any business venture you'd like to start. The magic words here are "sophisticated investor." Every successful professional – such as a doctor or lawyer – likes to think of himself or herself as sophisticated. And you can often attract these people to invest in your business.

Run an ad in your local paper, high-lighting those two key words.

Other magic phrases to include are "Local business person with excellent track record and reputable history"; start-up business opportunity, limited investment, high potential return"; and "references available."

Magic Phrase #2 – Receive Free Expert Help for your business. Simply announce "I have a business problem and need expert assistance," either to a local business group (such as the Chamber of Commerce, which you have in practically every town) or putting an advertisement in the business section of your local newspaper. And I've been absolutely delighted with the quality of assistance provided to me on several occasions by retired executives. Seek them out in your local area, and you could benefit from this great source of experienced know-how, too.

Magic Phrase #3 – Get Capable People to Work for Free. Your magic words here are "piece of the action." Instead of paying a fixed salary, run ads offering people one of these options:

- Hourly rate for services rendered
- Percentage of sales
- Percentage of profits
- Royalty on sales

- Percentage of savings
- Fixed payment for each unit produce

Anyone with a strong entrepreneurial instinct will be attracted by such an approach. It means there will be no limit on their income, they will be more independent, they can set their own hours – and the harder they work, the more they earn. This is just the type of person you should employ.

Assume The Other Person Has Already Said "Yes"

Ask questions which assume the end result you seek. For example, speaking with your bank manager about setting up a merchant account, you might ask these questions:

1. "How long does it normally take for a credit card charge to be credited to my account?"
2. "What discount or percentage of credit card sales will the bank charge us for your service?"
3. "How long would it take to get the service in place?"

4. "What equipment do we need to buy to make it easier for your bank to process our orders?"

Can you see how the end result – having a merchant account so you can process the credit card orders – is assumed by the very words used in each question?

Magic Words Deliver Power
And this is especially true when you're speaking to yourself. As I said at the beginning of this letter, I use affirmations every day – standing up, looking to the sky, throwing my hands in the air, and shouting out a positive message I need to tell myself.

Yes, I feel ridiculous when I do this too. But that discomfort is just the push I need to change my emotional state. The magic words in my affirmations give me the energy and determination I need to produce my very best work. And I truly believe they'll help you achieve your goals too.

Ted Nicholas, widely recognized as one of the greatest direct-marketing wizards of all time, is best-known for having earned 24.5 million dollars on the sale of a single book that was primarily sold through direct mail. He is called the Five Hundred Million Dollar Man because he has marketed over $500 million worth of products in 49 different industries. Ted's newest book, "Magic Words That Bring You Riches" reveals 17 magic words that can make you a fortune. For immediate access visit: www.davidlhancock.com/magicwords

The Secret Behind Million-Dollar Ads

Want a little secret to turn your advertising into an irresistible magnet for customers?

Dale Carnegie knew the secret, and that's one reason his book "How to Win Friends and Influence People" has sold more than 15 million copies. In fact, British Airways recently named it, "The Business Book of the 20th Century."

It's a great book. But if Dale had titled it "How to Remember People's Names and Curb Your Incessant Urge to Argue," do you think it would have sold as well? Probably not. There's great power in good titles.

What you may not realize is the words "How to Win Friends and Influence People" are not only the title of the book. Those words were also the headline of a mail-order ad, which sold the book. The ad ran successfully for many years and sold hundreds of thousands of copies.

So what does this have to do with turning your advertising into an irresistible customer magnet?

Here's what. Behind the title and headline is a "secret code" that makes it powerful. Dale knew it. Great advertising copywriters know it. And now, you're going to know it, too.

The "secret code" is actually a generic formula that gets attention and creates desire in your prospect's mind. Every winning headline has a unique generic formula hidden inside.

Here's the formula in Dale Carnegie's book title and headline:

How to _____ and _____.

Let's see the formula at work. Say you are an executive Recruiter, and you help companies find new executives. In reality, your biggest problem is finding the executive candidates in the first place. So, to increase your group of candidates, you decide to run an ad in your local business journal. Here's how you could use this formula to write a headline for your ad:

How to Get a Better Job and Make More Money

…and right away anyone who's even a little interested would read your ad. Then, if your copy (text) is even halfway decent, you'd get plenty of calls.

Or, let's say you run a martial arts school. Here's how you could apply the formula in an advertising headline to get you new students:

How to Stay Fit and Protect Yourself

Do you see how powerful that is? You've just zeroed-in on people who are likely to be interested in learning martial arts.

The brutal reality of advertising: An ad with a good headline, and even mediocre copy, will get you a response and generate sales. But with a poor headline, even the most brilliant copy will get you little or no response. Why? Because without a good headline to get their attention, most people won't read any further.

The good news is, once you have identified a good headline that works in one industry or market, you can adapt it (like we did with the Dale Carnegie headline, above) for your own business.

Great headlines work as subject lines in emails, titles on Web pages, and of course as headlines in print ads and sales letters. Great headlines will literally transform your sales.

How does this work in today's economy?

Recently a client asked David Garfinkel to help him introduce a new service to Internet Service Providers. (Note: To understand what you are about to read, you should know that ISPs call their suppliers "backbone providers.") He wrote a direct mail letter and my client sent it out to ISPs. Because his client was revealing new information his prospects hadn't heard before, they used the following "teaser headline" on the front of the envelope:

What Your Backbone Provider Isn't Telling You

Was this an entirely original headline? No. He had seen a similar "teaser headline" on a successful mailing to promote an investment newsletter:

What Your Broker Isn't Telling You About High-Tech Stocks

So he merely identified the "secret code" in the original winning headline, and applied it to my client's market, ISPs.

The response to the mailing was overwhelming! Nearly 10% of the entire ISP industry responded to their letter – and his client has added eight figures of new annual revenues as a result of the business that developed.

He's telling us this not to brag, but to point out the awesome power of good headlines. While many people spend hours and hours trying to come up with "the perfect headline" for their ads, there is an easier way. Find proven headlines that already work for another business in another industry, and adapt them to your business.

Then prepare for a flood of new customers! Learn more at: www.davidlhancock.com/headlines

David Garfinkel has been described as, "The world's greatest copywriting coach". He's a successful results oriented copywriter and the author of Advertising Headlines That Make You Rich, which shows you exactly how to adapt proven money-making headlines to your business. www.davidlhancock.com/headlines

DAVID L. HANCOCK

50 Benefits of Joint Venture Marketing!

What Is A Joint Venture?

A joint venture is an agreement in which two or more businesses work on a project for a set period of time. Joint ventures can be long-term, like promoting a product together, or some can be short-term, like bartering (trading) products and services. Joint venture ideas are virtually endless.

The Benefits of Joint Venture Marketing

1. You can build long lasting business relationships.
2. You can increase your credibility by teaming up with other reputable, branded businesses.
3. You can get free products and services.
4. You can construct most joint venture deals with little or no money.
5. You can gain new leads and customers.
6. You can get discounts on products and services.
7. You can save money on business operating costs.
8. You can beat your competition.
9. You can gain referrals from other businesses.
10. You can solve your business problems.
11. You can save valuable time.
12. You can get free and low cost advertising.
13. You can offer your customers new products and services.
14. You can survive a depression, recession or a slow economy.
15. You can save money by sharing advertising and marketing costs.

16. You can target other potential markets.
17. You can expand and grow your business quickly.
18. You can gain valuable information or skills.
19. You can increase and protect your cash flow.
20. You can find new profit outlets.
21. You can become rich and wealthy.
22. You can start almost any business at little or no costs.
23. You can get rid of your extra inventory.
24. You can reduce and eliminate your debts and avoid bankruptcy.
25. You can afford to sell your products at a lower price.
26. You can increase your opt in or e-zine subscribers for free.
27. You can get your web hosting and design for free.
28. You can save money outsourcing your workload for free.
29. You can find hidden income streams.
30. You can exchange useless products for profitable ones.
31. You can create new business funding and credit lines.

32. You can reduce your taxes.
33. You can find and create new distribution channels for your products.
34. You can give your employees more raises, bonuses and benefits.
35. You can even trade non business stuff to improve your personal life.
36. You can increase your sales and profits.
37. You can send your ad to huge, targeted email lists at no cost.
38. You can eliminate employee hiring costs creating barter outsourcing deals.
39. You can build your customer or opt-in list for free.
40. You can build profitable alliances with other businesses.
41. You can learn insider information from other experts at no cost.
42. You can test your product for free.
43. You can out-sell other affiliates much easier.
44. You can increase the number of affiliates that sign up to your reseller program.
45. You can offer more bonus products and incentives to buy.

46. You can get highly credible endorsements and testimonials from other experts.
47. You can quickly increase your e-zine subscribers.
48. You can offer your products at lower prices than your competition.
49. You can easily find new up sell and backend products to sell.
50. You can create products faster and with less effort.

These are only some of the benefits. They're endless!

For more in depth information, I recommend "How To Write Hypnotic Joint Ventures Proposals." by Larry Dotson. For immediate access visit: www.davidlhancock.com/jointventures

DAVID L. HANCOCK

The Strange Story of the "Crackpot" Mail-Order Prophet

Are you having trouble selling your product or service? Are you feeling like the chaotic state of the world prevents you from succeeding? Are you wondering how you can increase your sales in the most cost effective ways? Are you feeling like your competition is breathing down your neck?

Many of my clients feel the same way. They want to succeed, to make a nice living in their business, but they feel overwhelmed, uncertain, and even despondent. They feel they have too much competition. They feel marketing doesn't work, or takes too much work. They feel people don't have enough money today to spend on what they are selling.

And that's why I think it's time to reveal the strange story of the long forgotten "crackpot" mail-order prophet.

During the Great Depression of the 1930s the average person didn't have enough money to feed themselves or their family, let alone enough extra cash to order books through the mail. Yet during those lean years one man made a fortune selling books and courses entirely by mail. His name was Frank B. Robinson. He founded "Psychiana," the world's eighth largest religion and the world's largest mail-order religion.

You may never have heard of him or his movement before today. But during the 1930s and 40s, Robinson's name traveled around the world. Millions of people read his books, studied his lessons, and practiced his methods. The press called his positive thinking, new thought religion a "media business" because Robinson advertised so heavily.

In 1928 Robinson wrote an ad for his new philosophy that began with the headline, "I TALKED WITH GOD." An advertising agency in Spokane, Washington said the ad would never work. But Frank believed in his message and trusted his hunches. He borrowed $2,500 from people he barely knew, spent most of it on printing his lessons, and invested $400 to place his ad in "Psychology Magazine."

That ad pulled 5,300 responses. Robinson ran it in numerous magazines and it always pulled a 3% to 21% response. Within a year he had a full-time job fulfilling requests for his books and lessons, soon shipping a million pieces of mail a year out of his office in Moscow, Idaho. The post office in that little town had to move into a bigger building to handle all the mail.

Robinson's ads appeared in 140 newspapers, 180 magazines, and on 60 radio stations, all at the same time. His postal bill in 1938 amounted to $16,000 and his printing bill hit $40,000. He received 60,000 pieces of mail a day, reached more than two million people, and sent his message to 67 countries---all within one year of running his first ad.

"Advertising is educating the public to who you are, where you are, and what service you have to offer," Robinson wrote. "The only man or organization who should not advertise is the one who has nothing to offer."

What can we learn from Frank B. Robinson?

1. He believed in his product. When you don't believe in what you are trying to sell, it shows. It'll show in your lack of commitment to your marketing, in poor advertising, in poor service, or in other ways. As I mention in my book, The Seven Lost Secrets of Success, sincerity is one of the "lost secrets" to success. Robinson had sincerity. While his movement made tons of money, Robinson accepted only $9,000 a year as his salary. Whether you call him a crackpot or a savior, he believed in his product. He

knew he had something people wanted. In fact, Robinson sold his religious lessons with a money-back guarantee.

2. He advertised relentlessly. If you don't tell people that you exist, they won't know it. The reason you aren't aware of Robinson or his movement today is because he's dead. (He died in 1948). No one is advertising his message. Without consistent and persistent advertising to educate the public, the world won't know of your business.

3. He tracked his results. Robinson believed in the spiritual world, but he also knew he lived on the earth plane where numbers matter. He tracked responses from his ads to know what worked and what didn't. For example, astrology magazines brought him an 18% response to his ads while national weekly papers brought 3%. Knowing that, Robinson could invest more money in larger ads in the better pulling magazines. Find out where your business comes from and focus more advertising in that area.

4. He continued to create products. Robinson knew once people tasted his goods, they would want more. He wrote 28 books during his short lifetime. These, along with his correspondence courses, gave him a deep product line. Your current satisfied customers will always be your goldmine. Create more for them to buy.

5. He remained optimistic. Despite the harsh reality of the Great Depression years, and despite competition from religious institutions that had been around for centuries, Robinson flourished. He didn't believe anyone or anything could stop him. When you have that strong of an inner conviction, nothing CAN stop you. If you think you have competition with a similar business in the same town, consider what it must have been like for Robinson to have such empires as the Catholic Church, the US government, and famous ministers and politicians trying to close him down!

Whatever you may think of Robinson or "Psychiana," you have to admit he knew how to advertise his business.

"After all, it's the results in human lives that count," he wrote in his 1941 book, The Strange Autobiography of Frank B. Robinson. "Talk is cheap."

What are you going to do now to increase your business? Remember, talk is cheap!

Joe Vitale is widely recognized by many as the greatest copywriter in America. Can you beat him? Try out the "World's Shortest Advertising IQ Test" and see how you stack up:
www.davidlhancock.com/iqtest

DAVID L. HANCOCK

How to Close More Online Sales Through the Magic of Questions

No one can deny that sales closing techniques are absolutely vital in face-to-face selling. But often, people ask me if they can apply my powerful closing techniques to online marketing. My answer is an unequivocal, "Yes!"

Of course, there are some closing techniques that are more applicable to the Web than others -- but I'll show you magical closing secrets that can dramatically increase your web sales, and rapidly increase your online income. This works best on direct response websites - i.e., those that focus on getting an immediate response in the form of an order or lead.

Before we get started, I must emphasize that much of the sale is made in the presentation. The close is largely determined by how well you've presented the product to the prospect. Your objective, then, is to take the prospect smoothly past the point of closing, making it easy for him or her to come to a buying decision. You can accomplish this with the strategic use of questions.

The All-Important Opening Question

When you're selling online, you don't have the benefit of interacting with your prospect the way you would in face-to-face selling. Therefore, the first thing you say in your web copy has to be something that breaks preoccupation, grabs attention, and points to the result or benefit of your product.

At any given moment, your prospect's mind is preoccupied with dozens of things. Therefore, a well-crafted question will cause the prospect's thinking to be directed to what you have to say.

Your opening question must be aimed at something that is relevant and important, and at something that your prospect needs or wants. What do sales managers, for instance, sit around and think about all day long? Increasing sales! Therefore, if your target market consists of sales managers, here's an example of a question you can use as a headline or as the first part of your copy: "How would you like to see a method that would enable you to increase your sales by 20% to 30% over the next 12 months?"

When you ask such a question, the first thing that pops into the mind of the prospect should be, "What is it?" - whereupon you've captured his or her attention, and you can then begin to articulate how your product or service can solve the need posed by the question.

Plan your opening question carefully. If your opening question fails to break your prospect's preoccupation and grab his attention, he will click away before giving you the opportunity to present your product or service.

Questions That Keep Them Involved

Questions are equally vital during the presentation, i.e., in the body of your web copy, for clearly explaining how your product or service solves your prospect's problem in an easy, fast, or cost-effective way. Therefore, install questions within your sales copy that capture attention. Keep your prospect involved, and keep his mind from wandering off in a different direction by using intriguing questions that grab his lapels and jerk him toward you. For the length of time that it takes a prospect to answer a question in his mind, you have his total attention. The prospect is drawn more and more into the sales process as your questioning proceeds. If your questions are logical, orderly and sequential, you can lead the prospect forward toward the inevitable conclusion to purchase your product or service.

Tip: Never say something if you can ask it instead! Think of how you can phrase your key selling points as questions. The person who asks questions has control!

Closing Questions that Presume the Sale

Just as questions are important at the beginning and the body of your web copy, they are even more vital at the end in gaining a commitment to action.

The key to asking a closing question is confident expectation. You must skillfully craft your question to convey that you confidently expect the prospect to say, "Yes" or to agree to the sale.

For example, you can pose the following question in your web copy: "When would you like to start using <NAME OF YOUR PRODUCT HERE> to multiply your profits?" In other words, you don't ask if they want to buy your product, but when. This way, you're asking for the sale expectantly, and the more confidently you expect to sell, the more likely it is that you will sell.

Tip: In crafting your closing question, include the benefit that your prospect will get from your product.

When you ask a compelling closing question, you diffuse the tension that normally creeps up on your prospect at the "moment of truth." A prospect's tension leads to the hesitance that kills so many sales - both online and offline.

To be truly persuasive in the selling process, learn to use questions judiciously throughout your web copy. Instead of trying to overwhelm your prospects with reasons and rationales for doing what you want them to do, ask strategic questions instead. When you take the time to plan the wording of your questions, your prospect will become more interested in your product -- and consequently, you will make more sales.

Brian Tracy is a million-dollar master of peak sales performance and personal success strategies. As the world-renowned creator of 300 video and audio learning programs, and the best-selling author of 16 books, his ideas and approaches are used by most of the big money makers and the

superstars of selling. In his Real Video course, "24 Techniques for Closing the Sale," Brian shows you powerful tactics that can double or triple your sales closing rate -- and teach you how to sell 50% to 100% of all prospects that you come in contact with -- all in just 63 minutes.
www.davidlhancock.com/questions

DAVID L. HANCOCK

The Craziest Internet Business Idea in History

So, you've got a great Internet business idea. Yeah, I'm talking to you. You know who you are. You have this great idea that you love to brag about. You tell all of your friends how it's going to make you a millionaire.

And to you, oh great generator of ideas, I say:
So what!

I know (literally) hundreds of people that come up with million dollar ideas on a daily basis. I can count on my hands, however, the number of those people that have actually achieved a respectable level of success with those ideas.

What about you? Are you sitting there feeling good about yourself with that great idea of yours or are you actually doing something about it?

Now, before you answer that question, be honest with yourself about what you want. Some people, it seems, are satisfied just having people pat them on the back for having such a great idea.

What about you? Is the pat on the back enough? If so, stop reading right now. I'm just going to waste your time if that is the case.

However, if you're one of the elite few that genuinely has what it takes to turn that idea into money, read on.

--- *Point of No Return Starts Here* ---

Still with me? OK, then. Let's get started.

1. Pick one idea.

Decide right now that you want to turn this idea into money and try not to get bogged down in other ideas.

You're going to come up with hundreds of other ideas before you see this one to completion. Resist the temptation to treat all of them equally. You will be tempted to pursue every single idea you have. This is the kiss of death. You need to narrow your focus. That's the key to success.

2. Stop rationalizing.

Somewhere along the way you're going to say to yourself: "This idea isn't working, because it's not the best idea. I should have picked another."

Rubbish! This is the lazy part of your mind trying to give you an excuse for quitting.

Don't quit. You don't know that the "other idea" is better. You *can't* know this.

Drive on.

3. It's the marketing, stupid.

You should spend more of your time marketing than on any other task. In the course of running your business, it's easy to get caught up in a million idiotic things.

For example: "Which color paint do you think would look best in the ladies room? Pink or mauve?"

Who cares! Make little decisions quickly, or pass them to someone else.

If you are not spending 90% of your working day on marketing, something is wrong.

Fix it!

Now, you can say to yourself: "Of course he's right - I don't need you to tell

me all these things" and then forget
everything I've said.

Or, you can get started right now. I
think you know which path leads to wealth
and success. The question is, do you really
want it?

Mark Joyner is widely recognized as
one of the top Internet Marketing experts in
the world. His latest product, the Promote-
Ivator, is an amazing little app that will give
your Internet business a much needed kick
in the tail:
The Promote-Ivator
www.davidlhancock.com/promote-ivator

DAVID L. HANCOCK

What is Marketing in the First Place?

Marketing is a process, not an event. Marketing is absolutely every bit of contact any part of your business has with any segment of the public. Guerrillas view marketing as a circle that begins with your ideas for generating revenue and continues on with the goal of amassing a large number of repeat and referral customers. The three keys words in that paragraph are EVERY, REPEAT, and REFERRAL. If your marketing is not a circle, it's a straight line that leads directly into Chapters 7, 11, or 13 in the bankruptcy courts.

HOW IS GUERRILLA MARKETING DIFFERENT FROM TRADITIONAL MARKETING?

Guerrilla marketing means marketing that is unconventional, non- traditional, not by-the-book, and extremely flexible. Eighteen factors make it different from old-fashioned marketing:

1. Instead of investing money in the marketing process, you invest time, energy, and imagination.
2. Instead of using guesswork in your marketing, you use the science of psychology, laws of human behavior.
3. Instead of concentrating on traffic, responses, or gross sales, profits are the only yardstick by which you measure your marketing.
4. Instead of being oriented to companies with limitless bank accounts, guerrilla marketing is geared to small business.

5. Instead of ignoring customers once they've purchased, you have a fervent devotion to customer follow-up.

6. Instead of intimidating small business owners, guerrilla marketing removes the mystique from the entire marketing process, clarifies it.

7. Instead of competing with other businesses, guerrilla marketing preaches the gospel of cooperation, urging you to help others and let them help you.

8. Instead of trying to make sales, guerrillas are dedicated to making relationships, for long-term relationships are paramount in the nineties.

9. Instead of believing that single marketing weapons such as advertising work, guerrillas know that only marketing combinations work.

10. Instead of encouraging you to advertise, guerrilla marketing provides you with 100 different marketing weapons; advertising is only one of them.

11. Instead of growing with an idea of diversifying, guerrilla marketing

suggests that you grow if you want, but be sure to maintain your focus.

12. Instead of aiming your message at groups, guerrilla marketing encourages you to aim it at individuals.

13. Instead of counting up sales at the end of each month, guerrillas count up new relationships; know that they are the foundation of increased sales.

14. Instead of thinking of what they can take from customers and prospects, guerrillas think of what they can give. In the information age, they freely give information.

15. Instead of avoiding technology, guerrillas embrace it. If they are techno phobic, they make an appointment with a techno shrink. Technophobia is fatal these days.

16. Instead of being haphazard and unintentional all guerrilla marketing is intentional, from how the phone is answered to the attire guerrillas wear.

17. Instead of talking about yourself and being "me" marketing, guerrilla marketing talks about the customer and is "you" marketing.

18. Instead of going for the sale with marketing, guerrilla marketing goes for consent to receive marketing materials, then only markets to those who have given their consent.

These are 18 very critical differences and are probably the reasons that the concept of guerrilla marketing has filled a void in the world's economy, explaining why the guerrilla books have been translated into 37 languages, sold over one million copies, are required reading in most MBA programs, are available in audiotape and videotape versions, as computer software, as a nationally-syndicated column, as a newsletter, and are the most popular and widely-read marketing books in the world.

The essence of guerrilla marketing boils down to a blend of common sense, realistic expectations, and a fervent commitment to a plan. It is hardly a miracle worker, but when accomplished properly, does seem to work miracles for those with the patience, aggressiveness and willingness to constantly learn. These days, marketing success does not belong to those who learn everything about anything, but to those who learn one thing after another. Learning about marketing and guerrilla marketing is the best place to start if you are to become a master of marketing.

Jay Conrad Levinson is probably the most respected marketer in the world. He is the inventor of "Guerrilla Marketing" and is responsible for some of the most outrageous marketing campaigns in history -- including the "Marlboro Man" -- the most successful ad campaign in history. In his latest book, "Put Your Internet Marketing on Steroids," Jay reveals how you can use marketing steroids legally to make your business insanely profitable.
Find out more at
www.davidlhancock.com/steroids

Until now, no marketing association in existence could make a business bulletproof. But once again, Jay Conrad Levinson, the most respected marketer in the world, has broken new ground. The Guerrilla Marketing Association is quite literally a blueprint for business immortality. You've got to have it!

Join right now before your competition does! www.davidlhancock.com/gma

DAVID L. HANCOCK

Three Ways to Get Repeat Sales with Follow-up Marketing

If you have customers, that's good.

If you can sell them repeatedly over time, that's better!

Actively pursuing repeat sales, also known as backend sales, is one of the most profitable things you can do for your small business.

Here are three ways to do it...

1. Say, "Thank you".

Start with a simple thank-you letter. Ask yourself this: "When's the last time you got a thank-you letter from a company after giving them your money?" I'll bet you can't remember. See the possibilities for standing out and generating good will?

I created an email template so I don't have to write the same thank-you email over and over. It literally takes seconds for me to send one out to each client.

A heartfelt "thank you" is all you really have to say, but you can go a bit further in your message, by doing the following:

✓ Reinforce why it was a good idea to buy from you in the first place - sell your company after the sale to cut down on buyer's remorse and returns/refunds.

✓ Offer another product or service to complement their original purchase;

you can make this a limited-time offer, as I do.

✓ Refer customers to affiliate programs at other Web sites that pay you anticipate frequently asked questions (FAQ) and tell customers how they can get service after the sale.

✓ Ask for referrals.

Simply sending a thank-you message after the sale will help nip service problems in the bud. By acknowledging people who buy from you and opening a channel of communication, you can turn unhappy customers into raving fans who later recommend your business.

Really, when you think of it, the only thing that differentiates your business (online or off) is service.

Yes, it's crucial to have the highest-quality product/service possible. But what customers remember (and what they tell their friends) is how they were treated. You can set the tone for a positive, profitable relationship with all your customers simply by thanking them right after they purchase from you.

2. Send a survey.

Customer feedback, negative or positive, is a crucial tool for fixing holes in your business. You can get that feedback via an online survey.
As of this writing, you can get one free at Zoomerang (www.zoomerang.com). I've used them for over a year and highly recommend their survey creator.

A good customer survey is like a vigorous massage - you may feel beat up after reading the results, because NO business serves its customers as well as it thinks it does, but the results will energize you.

A survey is a window into your clients' minds. If you include a section for them to include their comments, it's like having a free product research laboratory! LISTEN and ACT on what your customers tell you. They'll give you invaluable tips on what new products to sell, joint ventures to form, etc.

You'll also find that clients answering your survey will often give you testimonials, which you can later use on your Web site. As you probably know, testimonials are an incredibly effective way to boost credibility and sales.

I've accumulated five or six pages of them over the years (I stopped counting) and prospects continually tell me that my testimonials were a deciding factor in why they chose to buy from me.

3. Introduce them to non-competitors' products.

What if customers won't need your product/service again for a long time, if ever? If you haven't done so already, set up affiliate deals from other Web sites that offer items related to your own.

My business offers a perfect example. Buying a resume is a lot like visiting the dentist -- it's not something people look forward to, and they likely won't make a repeat purchase for 6-12 months… or longer.

To overcome this, I email my clients information about career-related Web sites where they can register for job search services, buy books and audio tapes refer jobs to friends, etc. Each of these sites has an affiliate program that pays me every time people register or buy. It all adds up to hundreds of dollars in monthly revenue that would have been left on the table had I not introduced my customers to these other sites.

Need ideas on what kinds of products or services to offer your customers? You can search for an affiliate program that's right for your customers in my "Resources" section

Author Kevin Donlin has been selling online since 1995. This article is an excerpt from "How to Double Your Small Business Sales in 20 Minutes a Day with Follow-up Marketing", a new manual that does just what the title says. Guaranteed. To learn more, visit:
www.davidlhancock.com/follow-up

Resources:

Here are some of the resources I use every day in my quest to be the best:

- o 33 Days to Online Profits – The step-by-step, day-by-day guide to finally making real money online in 33 days or less for almost any product or service you sell. www.davidlhancock.com/33days

- o 33 days to Online Profits VIDEO Enhanced Tutorial eBook – Updated and revised version of "33 days" with screen capture video Jam-packed on 2 CD-ROM's this goes way beyond e-books, beyond membership sites… or anything else before it! 41 videos totaling 3 hours, 9 minutes, and 44 seconds of video instruction from Yanik and Jim. www.davidlhancock.com/33daysvideo

o 5-Minute PDF Creator – Perfect tutorial resource for anyone that wants to quickly and easily create great looking e-books and any other digital content. Over 150 screen captures, diagrams and full color graphics, really gives you exact step-by-step details for publishing success. www.davidlhancock.com/pdf

o ad-CLiX Viral Web Traffic Generation – FREE to join – Earn ad credits for every ad you show (Exit pop-under and Banner Ad) and every ad shown by members below you (4 more levels). New members joining with no referral link are allocated to your x by 4-tier network. www.davidlhancock.com/ad-clix

- AdMinder – If you have ever promoted ANYTHING online and you ended up losing money, or didn't make as much as you had expected ... then check out AdMinder to discover a GUARANTEED solution. www.davidlhancock.com/adminder

- Adobe – Free Reader: Streamline document-based processes to enhance productivity, improve customer service, and increase profits. www.adobe.com

- Advanced Copywriting Seminar-in-a-box – Only 115 people were permitted to attend Dan Kennedy's recent, closed door, 2-day Seminar where he revealed ALL of his most prized, most powerful and most profitable copywriting techniques. Everything else was just "elementary school" before this. www.davidlhancock.com/copy

- Affiliate Cash Flow Marketing - David L. Hancock, The Marketing Master™ & Author Says "Now You

Can Have All The Money You Want"
Using His New System. David has
created A Dirt Cheap Marketing
System That Makes Ordinary
Affiliates Top Producers in 12-18
Months! Learn How to Stop Wasting
Time & Position Yourself Now!
www.AffiliateCashFlowMarketing.co
m

o Affiliate Mistakes – 10 mistakes that
  are keeping you from making $100,
  $200, or more each day from affiliate
  programs!
  www.davidlhancock.com/mistakes

o AffiliateShowcase – Free: Affiliate
  Showcase is a fantastic viral system
  that automatically grows leads and
  gives you your own Affiliate
  Directory Site with the ability to
  display hundreds of your own custom
  referral links!
  www.davidlhancock.com/showcase

o Amazon.com – Opened its virtual
  doors in July 1995 with a mission to
  use the Internet to transform book
  buying into the fastest, easiest, and

most enjoyable shopping experience possible.
www.davidlhancock.com/amazon

o Autoresponder Magic –
Autoresponder Magic is a massive collection of winning autoresponder messages to model, copy and swipe from the top Internet marketers around.
www.davidlhancock.com/magic

o BizMint – Offers an extremely unique approach to finding quality domain names, powerfully branding a website and increasing sales.
www.davidlhancock.com/bizmint

o ClickBank – Accept credit cards on your site without the hassle of a merchant account. Plus, introduce your own affiliate program to drive traffic to your site using ClickBank's affiliate management services.
www.davidlhancock.com/clickbank

o DynamiteCovers – Free: Maximize your clickthroughs, downloads and sales and drive up to 317% more

customer actions on your website, when you tantalize prospects with a professional-looking, three-dimensional cover or box. Make your product look so real that people will reach out into their computer screens and grab it!
www.davidlhancock.com/dynamitecovers

o eBook Generator - Become an Instant Author. You can now create your very own eBooks in less time than it takes to make a cup of coffee.
www.davidlhancock.com/ebookgenerator

o eBookGold – offering Internet marketers one of the most Powerful e-Publishing tools on the market.
www.davidlhancock.com/ebookgold

o eCover Generator - The Internet's First eCover Software. Why spend hundreds of dollars on 3D covers and software box images, when you can make them yourself in a few short minutes.
www.davidlhancock.com/ecover

o FrontPage Tools – FrontPage Tools, Training and Templates Made by

people who use FrontPage to run their business.
www.davidlhancock.com/frontpage

o GetResponse – Free: New, sophisticated autoresponder allows fast, repetitive, personalized and consistent email follow-up. SAVE time and money! GRAB YOUR FREE VERSION NOW! Grab a FREE bonus report: "How to Double Your Sales With a Proper Email Strategy"!
www.davidlhancock.com/getresponse

o Header Generator - 300+ Hand Crafted header graphics with a built in graphical editor to create your own header graphics for your website.
www.davidlhancock.com/header

o Home Business Connection – Free: Magazine shows you how to start your own business from home. Request a FREE copy of Home Business Connection Magazine.
www.davidlhancock.com/hbc

o   HyperTracker – Free: Never lose a dime in lost advertising revenue again! Our ingenious tool will track and monitor all of your campaigns, and tell you which advertising campaigns are bringing in the sales, whilst the rest are just useless hits.
www.davidlhancock.com/hypertracker

o   Instant Internet Profits – This course shows a completely different approach to Internet marketing.
www.davidlhancock.com/profits

o   Instant Marketing Toolbox – Turn-key, monthly marketing system with over 90% of the hard work already done for you... If you're too busy running your business to even think about marketing – this is what you've been waiting for.
www.davidlhancock.com/toolbox

o   Instant Sales Letters – Instant Sales Letter templates are a valuable (and effective) marketing tool for nearly any business owner who wants to increase their profits. You can create your own powerful sales letter in just

minutes…without writing!
www.davidlhancock.com/letters

o Internet Marketing Lab Video set –
Sneak Away with the Exact Same
Online Moneymaking Tools and
Profit Strategies Revealed at the Sold-
Out $4,995.00/per person 'Internet
Marketing Lab' – for Just Pennies on
the Dollar!
www.davidlhancock.com/lab

o Ken Varga – Never before revealed
secrets from my newly released book,
How To Get Customers to Call, Buy
and Beg for More to get all the
customers you ever want and to
double your sales and bottom line
profits in less than one year.
www.davidlhancock.com/kenvarga

o Kevin Donlin - I'm fortunate enough
to know Kevin Donlin, author of the
"How to Double Your Small
Business Sales in 20 Minutes a Day
with Follow-up Marketing". He's
been marketing online since before
there was a Web. And the ideas I get
from him I take straight to the bank!

Kevin teaches marketing tactics that have been endorsed by the likes of Jay Conrad Levinson, author of the Guerrilla Marketing series of books. www.davidlhancock.com/follow-up

o Lexington Law – Lexington is a law firm specializing in credit repair. They've helped over 80,000 Americans repair their credit by removing inaccurate, misleading, or unverifiable items from their credit reports. www.increaseyourscore.com

o Link Check Generator - Secret Software Tool Lets Any Average Joe Gain an Unfair Advantage Over Competition. www.davidlhancock.com/linkchecker

o Magnetic Marketing – Amazingly powerful advertising, marketing, direct marketing, customer / client attraction & persuasion strategies revealed! A complete business building package from Dan Kennedy. www.davidlhancock.com/magnetic

o   Make Your Knowledge Sell! - Turn knowledge into revenue. Sell your brain on the Internet. How to brainstorm, create, produce, and sell your own info product. www.davidlhancock.com/myks

o   Make Your Price Sell! - Price with complete confidence and double your Internet profits. "How much money are you leaving on the table?" www.davidlhancock.com/myps

o   Make Your Net Auction Sell! - An e-biz in every closet... Get into Auction Action! Start and grow a profitable Net auction business. www.davidlhancock.com/mynas

o   Make Your Site Sell! 2002 - The definitive work on making any Web site SELL! Widely acknowledged as "the bible of selling on the Net." www.davidlhancock.com/myss

o   Make Your Words Sell! - Want to sell more? Use better words... much better. Become an e-persuader. www.davidlhancock.com/myws

o Million Dollar Emails – Million Dollar Emails reveals the secrets of using email marketing and the power to create cash on demand. Imagine, anytime you need more money, you just hit SEND! Click…Send…Make Money! www.davidlhancock.com/million

o Mining Gold On The Internet – Shawn Casey has developed several very successful Websites that bring in a ton of money. More importantly, he's built them all without spending a lot of money on marketing. He specializes in no-cost and low-cost strategies that anyone can use. www.davidlhancock.com/mininggold

o NameStick – New service for affiliate marketers allows you to dramatically increase the results you receive promoting affiliate programs (more clicks and more sales) by as much as 327%. Finally, you never have to use a long, ugly, ineffective affiliate domain link ever again. www.davidlhancock.com/namestick

o   PayPal – Free: The easiest and cheapest way for small businesses and websites to accept payments online. #1 payment service on eBay. Trusted on over 5 million auctions. www.davidlhancock.com/paypal

o   PopUp Generator - With Resell Rights - Creates popups for your website instantly with a simple to use interface that will save you boatloads of time and energy. www.davidlhancock.com/popup

o   Power Pause - In just three minutes, with only 3 steps, you can achieve personal success and real happiness. Not only do the three steps work, but you can do them anywhere, anytime, for any situation. www.davidlhancock.com/powerpause

o   ROIbot – Free: The Roibot affiliate program covers many products from software to eBooks and is a 2 tier program. Something for all online marketers. www.davidlhancock.com/roibot

o Sales Letter Generator - Create perfectly formatted sales letters in a matter of minutes. Have your own 24 hour world class copywriter at your fingertips.
www.davidlhancock.com/saleslettergenerator

o Site Build It! – "Why build JUST a Web site when you COULD build a Web BUSINESS?"
www.davidlhancock.com/sitebuildit

o Site Sell! - Since 1997, SiteSell.com books and software have empowered over 100,000 entrepreneurs and small businesses to outperform larger, well-financed competitors. They will do the same for you.
www.davidlhancock.com/sitesell

o SiteSell 5 Pillar Affiliate Registration - Award-winning affiliate program from Ken Evoy that includes the following products. With a large number of free courses and other re-branded downloads to use as presales tools. As an affiliate, you earn a commission of between 25 & 30% of each sale promoting highly acclaimed and affordable, marketing products. www.davidlhancock.com/5pillar

o Six-Figure Income Marketing Group (SFI) – Free: Sign up for top-rated Free Affiliate Program with over 7 million SFI affiliates worldwide! www.gosixfigureincome.com

o Stamps.com – Free: Make the mailing process easy and seamlessly integrates with your database. Get up to $25 in Free Postage. www.davidlhancock.com/stamps

o Surefire Marketing – Surefire Marketing is Yanik Silvers site for promotion of "a Whole Slew of Best-Selling Products". www.davidlhancock.com/letters

o Winning the Affiliate Game – 25% on sales from your website – 10% from other sites you refer to us. That's right, we encourage you to set up your own affiliate network and earn 10% from all of their sales as

well as 25% of your own sales!
www.davidlhancock.com/winning

o Xerox – Free High Performance
   Color Printers. In an ongoing drive to
   remove prohibitive cost barriers to
   high speed color printing, Xerox
   created the Free Color Printers
   program which allows organizations
   access to powerful and fast color
   printers such as the remarkable
   Phaser series with absolutely no
   upfront capital investment.
   www.davidlhancock.com/xerox

It is my sincere hope that these master
marketing secrets will help you create
endless streams of new, repeat, and referral
business – they have for many others. I wish
you great success on your quest for
increased business!

David L. Hancock
The Marketing Master™

Like This Book? Want More?

Get Your Copy of Affiliate Cash Flow Marketing Now at www.AffiliateCashFlowMarketing.com the full On-line Marketing Manual!

Do it today and receive a Free Copy of Search Engine Primer so you can learn EXACTLY how you can drive MASSIVE amounts of traffic to your website! Plus much, much more!

About the Author...

David L. Hancock has been in marketing his entire life. He is an accomplished mortgage banker, speaker, author, entrepreneur and a professional affiliate that offers business-building solutions and e-commerce solutions for anyone who sell products or services online or off.

He has been an Internet marketer since 1995 and has helped thousands of people start and promote their own Internet businesses with over 120,000+ subscribers to his systems. He is known in the Industry as a Marketing Master and a major threat by his competitors.

David's business philosophy is to offer the absolute best tools and information available on the market in the most accessible format and at the most affordable price. David feels strongly that everyone can use the Internet to leverage their income-building potential - whether it's to build an e-business or a secondary income stream.

He resides in Virginia with his wife and two children.

DAVID L. HANCOCK

Printed in the United States
27631LVS00001B/1-9